Letts
EDUCATIONAL

KEY SKILLS LEVEL 3

Survival Guide

Key Skills

evel 3

...ation

Contents

5. Producing your portfolio of evidence 37

6. The external assessment 43

7. Answers 53

Appendices 60

1 An introduction to Key Skills 1

Key Skills are...

Generic skills that help to improve learning and performance in:

★ Education and training   ★ Work and life in general

They are important in:

★ learning   ★ career and   ★ personal life

Key Skills aim to...

Develop and recognise skills in:

- obtaining and interpreting different types of information
- using, developing and communicating information to meet the purpose of studies, work and other activities
- effectively presenting results

Curriculum 2000

From September 2000, if you are a Curriculum 2000 student, you will be aiming to achieve Key Skills units alongside your main programme of study. Just like any other subject, Key Skills need to be taught and developed before you can produce successful final evidence.

Key Skills will play an important part in widening your studies and experiences along with other initiatives, such as community service or any other 'enhancement' studies. You could also consider any full-time or part-time employment you have which could give you the opportunity to develop and evidence some of your skills.

You will be using many of the skills already without even realising it. Take a look at Appendix D (see page 69) where you will see the list of qualifications that you may already have and that could give you exemption(s) from some parts of the Key Skills Awards. (Make sure you ask your teachers for an up-to-date list. This one was current in June 2000.)

From 2000 onwards, many students will also use the opportunities presented by their Citizenship studies to develop and evidence their Key Skills. Every qualification you study from September 2000 will be sign-posted for its opportunities for Key Skills development and evidence.

HE, Key Skills and the world of work

- Higher Education institutions are working on developing the Key Skills of their students in order to make them more autonomous and effective learners.

- The points that will be awarded by UCAS for applicants for HE in September 2002 for each of the Key Skills (Communication, Application of Number and IT) will be as follows:

Level	UCAS points per unit
Level 4	30 points
Level 3	20 points
Level 2	10 points

(To see the specifications for Level 2 and Level 4 you can visit the QCA website on www.qca.org.uk)

- Employers have always loved Key Skills. They may not have called them that, but they constantly ask for people who can work both in a team and on their own. They want people who can quickly synthesise information and present it in an appropriate form. They like employees who are accurate with numbers and can use IT to enhance the content and presentation of their work.

'Key Skills are skills that are commonly needed for success in a range of activities in education and training, work and life in general. The Key Skills units aim to develop and recognise candidates' ability to apply these skills in ways that are appropriate to different contexts in order to improve the quality of learning and performance. They are intended for everyone, from pupils in school to chief executives in large companies.'
Guidance on the Key Skills Units, QCA (2000)

The individual Key Skills

From September 2000, new Key Skills will be launched. There are six Key Skills:

- **Communication (C)**
- **Information Technology (IT)**
- **Application of Number (N)**
- **Working with Others (WO)**
- **Improving own Learning and Performance (LP)**
- **Problem Solving (PS)**

- The first three are often known as the 'hard' or main Key Skills and the last three as the 'soft' or 'wider' Key Skills. This book will concentrate, along with the other two volumes in this series, on developing your 'hard' Key Skills. These are the three that will attract UCAS points.

- Each Key Skill has separate units up to and including Level 4. All the units for each level are presented in the same way. Level 5 is assessed by way of one single integrated unit.

Key Skills levels

Level 1	A student working at this level might be in the first year of a GCSE course or might achieve a D-G at GCSE.
Level 2	A student who is capable and able to gain A*-C at GCSE should be working at this level.
Level 3	Students working towards A/S, A Level and GNVQ/Vocational A Levels should be capable of this level in some or all of the Key Skills.
Level 4	Students working at undergraduate level should be developing skills at this level in some or all Key Skills.
Level 5	This is a managerial, postgraduate level and is gained by putting together a large body of evidence to demonstrate application of these high level skills. Note: generally you would need to be in a role/job that would allow you to demonstrate competence at this level, i.e. managerial or supervisory.

Not everyone will be at the same level in every Key Skill or wish to progress to the same level. You may feel that you will not need to achieve Level 3 in Application of Number to follow your career goal or you may find that IT at Level 2 is sufficient at the moment. Key Skills awards allow you to achieve at the level most appropriate for **you**, while giving you the chance to develop. It is always possible to pick up your Key Skills at a later stage and develop them further. **You should also bear in mind that some students will have chosen subject combinations at post-16 that give them more opportunities for Key Skills developments than others.**

It doesn't matter which awarding/examining body your school or college uses, as all the requirements for achieving your Key Skills are identical. Institutions may use the same awarding body, which will accredit your other qualifications, or they may choose one awarding body to accredit all their Key Skills candidates.

Where will my Key Skills evidence come from?

Your teachers and tutors will be working to make Key Skills attainments as straightforward as possible for you. A great deal of your evidence for the individual units will come from work that you undertake for your other subjects. You will also find that one piece of work can cover the requirements of more than one Key Skill, for example one essay may cover elements of Communication, IT, Working with Others and Problem Solving. It is important that you get to grips with the Unit Specifications – if you understand them well you can plan to get the maximum Key Skills material from each piece of work. In this way you will be gaining extra qualifications without giving yourself a great deal of extra work.

How are Key Skills assessed?

There are two elements to the assessment of Key Skills.

1. A **portfolio** of naturally occurring evidence which will be:

- **internally assessed** (by your tutors/teachers)

- **internally verified/moderated** (teachers check each others' marks to make sure they are all working to the same standards)

- **externally moderated** (by a representative from the awarding body to assure that all internal marking is to the standard required)

2. An **external assessment instrument** to assess:

- **knowledge/understanding**

- **externally set tasks**

You have to pass both of these elements in order to achieve your Key Skills unit(s). The Unit Specifications tell you everything you need to know in order to do this.

The Key Skills Qualification

Every Key Skill is available in its own right as a free-standing unit. But those students who achieve the **three** Key Skills – **Application of Number, Communication and Information Technology** – will receive a national certificate of units **and** the Key Skills Qualification.

It doesn't matter at what level you get the Key Skills, as they will be profiled, for example two at Level 3 and one at Level 2.

The Key Skills Qualification is a profile of achievement in three Key Skills units:

> **Portfolio and Test =**
> **COMMUNICATION**
> **+**
> **Portfolio and Test =**
> **APPLICATION OF NUMBER**
> **+**
> **Portfolio and Test =**
> **INFORMATION TECHNOLOGY**

Considering the wider Key Skills

The specifications for the three 'wider' Key Skills – **Working With Others (WO)**, **Improving Own Learning and Performance (LP) and Problem Solving (PS)** – identify the skills and competencies considered important to the worlds of study and employment, and for your personal development.

Your school or college may or may not enter students for the wider Key Skills: this does not mean that you should ignore them. Even if you are not aiming for a formal qualification in the wider Key Skills, you will find that you will benefit personally and academically if you aim to develop these skills and gain unit certification.

Working With Others (WO)

In school, college or in part-time employment, are there situations where you have to:

- agree objectives, who does what, when and how?
- organise your time and tasks in order to achieve what you have agreed?
- work co-operatively with others (even if you don't like them!)?
- review what you are doing and consider whether better ways of working can be devised?

Improving Own Learning and Performance (LP)

In school, college or part-time employment, are there situations where you have to:

- identify and agree targets and action plans yourself to meet these targets?
- follow your action plan and gain support and feedback from others when necessary to enable you to meet your targets?
- realistically review and assess your progress and provide evidence of this progress and your achievements?

Problem Solving (PS)

In school, college or part-time employment, do you ever have to:

- identify, consider and describe problems?
- identify and compare different ways in which you could solve problems?
- plan and put into place a solution?
- devise, agree and apply methods for checking that a problem has been solved and review approaches to tackling problems?

If you can say 'Yes' to any of these, have a close look at the Unit Specifications for the wider Key Skills at Level 3. You probably already have the potential to produce evidence that meets the specifications.

(For more details on the wider Key Skills, visit the QCA website at www.qca.org.uk)

These are the outlines of the requirements for each level of Communication:

Level 1	Level 2	Level 3	Level 4
Candidates must be able to: • take part in discussion about straightforward subjects • read and identify the main points and ideas from documents about straightforward subjects • write about straightforward subjects	Candidates must be able to: • help move discussions forward • give a short talk using an image to illustrate their points • read and summarise information from extended documents • use a suitable structure and style when writing extended documents	Candidates must be able to: • create opportunities for others to contribute to group discussions about complex subjects • make a presentation using a range of techniques to engage the audience • read and synthesise information from extended documents about a complex subject • organise information coherently, selecting a form and style of writing appropriate to complex subject matter	Candidates must be able to produce at least one extended example that requires them to: • develop a strategy for using communication skills over an extended period of time • monitor progress and adapt their strategy as necessary to achieve the quality of outcomes required in work, involving a group discussion and an extended written communication about a complex subject • evaluate their overall strategy and present outcomes from their work using a formal oral presentation with images

It may be useful for you to look at Levels 1 and 2 Communication as there is an expectation that if you can achieve Level 3 you can do everything required in Levels 1 and 2. Your teachers/tutors may be able to help but, if not, try having a look on the QCA (Qualifications and Curriculum Authority) website – the address is www.qca.org.uk

Getting started

- All the units for each Key Skill at every level, up to Level 4, are presented in the same way.

- Each Key Skill unit has a **Unit Specification**, which is divided into three parts:

PART A	A description of what the candidate needs to know
PART B	An outline of what candidates must do
PART C	Brief guidance on activities and examples of evidence

(If you haven't already seen a Key Skills specification, you will find the full specification for Communication Level 3 printed in Appendix A on pages 61–64.)

The first things you need to do are **read** the Unit Specification and **understand** what is required of you.

The Unit Specification tells you clearly what the unit is about. Communication Level 3 is about **applying your communication skills to a range of complex subjects**

and extended written materials. Acquiring these skills will enhance your performance in your other subjects.

There are two important words in the paragraph above that need further explanation:

COMPLEX – 'Complex subjects and materials present a number of ideas, some of which may be abstract, very detailed or require candidates to deal with sensitive issues. The relationship of ideas and lines of reasoning may not be immediately clear. Specialised vocabulary and complicated sentence structures may be used.'

EXTENDED – 'Extended documents include textbooks and reports, articles and essays of more than **three** pages. They may deal with straightforward or complex subjects and include images such as diagrams, pictures or charts. Candidates are asked to read extended documents at Level 2 and above to show, for example, that they can identify lines of reasoning in fairly lengthy material and structure their writing to help others follow their sequence of ideas.'
Guidance on the Key Skills Units, QCA (2000)

> In **PART A**, there are four main headings covering:
> > **Taking part in discussions**
> > **Making presentations**
> > **Reading and synthesising information**
> > **Writing documents**
> Part A prescribes the skills you will need to have or acquire in order to be successful at Level 3 Communication.

Taking part in discussions

Taking part in a discussion sounds a very grand title but it isn't really. Think about it – how often do you speak in a group or on a one-to-one basis during the day to give or exchange information? If you can do this, you are probably already working at Level 2. For Level 3 in Communication you will be expected to participate in a COMPLEX discussion and you will need opportunities to practise this.

- You need to be able to demonstrate that you contribute in a way that is relevant to the purpose and the subject, giving and obtaining information and exchanging ideas.

- Listening is an important skill that you must develop. Are you always sure that you have heard and understood what the other person has said?

- You also need to be sensitive to those people who do not find it easy to contribute and create opportunities for them to participate.

- These skills need to be learned, practised and demonstrated in a variety of settings and contexts.

- Think about how you talk to people you know and people you do not know – is there a difference?

- Do you always listen to others or are you always keen to be the loudest and make your point heard?

- Do you miss out on some good ideas and suggestions by not listening closely?

WIDENING OPPORTUNITIES FOR DEVELOPMENT

> **Do you think more widely than school or college when thinking about developing your discussion skills? Do you have a part-time job where you deal with people who want to make a complaint? Do you participate in a hobby where meetings are necessary to make decisions?**

This range of skills will be assessed as a part of your PORTFOLIO of evidence, which we will discuss later in the book.

Making presentations

Most of you will have had experience of making presentations during your English GCSE oral work but at Key Skills Level 3 the nature of the presentation is intended to be more formal.

Your approach to a presentation should be similar to writing an essay: you need to plan and structure, supporting ideas with IMAGES, which can include charts, diagrams or any visual aids you think appropriate.

Language and style

- Language and style need close attention, including any specialist vocabulary, which may need additional explanations for your audience.

- Above all, you must not read from a script – it is very boring for the audience and generally means that you have no confidence in the work you have prepared.

Polishing your performance

- To some extent making presentations is a 'performance' skill. To some people this comes quite naturally but others suffer with horrendous nerves and consider taking the day off sick! You know who you are and, if you ask around, some of your friends who always seem so confident are actually 'faking it'. Eventually you do not have to pretend – the confidence will come.

- Presenting your ideas to others and persuading them of the merits of your point of view or ideas is a really crucial skill that can have huge benefits in employment later. It is not about bullying but about reasoned argument.

This is another of the skills of Communication that will be assessed through your PORTFOLIO.

Reading and synthesising information

During your time as a student and later on in your world of work, there is no doubt that you will frequently feel under pressure to produce work to deadlines. Unfortunately, this is quite natural and unlikely to change! However, there are certain things that you can do to ease that pressure.

Focusing your reading

- Many people spend hours or even days plodding through books, magazines, even websites which are not going to be of use to them in their essay, report etc. One of the quickest ways to save time is to develop the skills of skimming and selection of information.

- Think of your purpose and work towards it.

Tone and style

- You must learn to read texts and to identify the tone of the writing – is it factual or is it emotive (a piece of writing trying to persuade the reader to the writer's point of view)? Sometimes this is very confusing, especially in newspapers or on TV where fact and fiction are often blurred. With practice you will be able to be a critical reader and make up your own mind. You need to recognise the purpose of texts from the author's style.

Referencing

- You must also remember that whenever you use other people's words or ideas, you must acknowledge this. If you do not, you leave yourself open to accusation of plagiarism, in blunt terms 'copying'. This may be unintentional but it is a crucial issue and we will discuss referencing others' work later on in this book.

Writing documents

Key Skills Communication evidence may require you to write in a style or to a format that is new to you. When producing written material, you are required to select the format most appropriate to your task: it may be an essay or a report; it could include a formal business letter or a memo. Most of these come with a 'standard' style and can be learned. We will discuss some of them later on.

To use IT or not?

- IT has improved the presentation of many students' work and has encouraged the use of bold type, underlining and paragraphing to improve the way work 'looks'. You need to consider if this also improves the way a piece of writing 'reads'. Whether you are word processing or handwriting your work, think of it like a map. Can the reader find their way around your work, can they follow your ideas and is the structure logical?

Spelling, punctuation and grammar

- A really crucial part of this section is the matter of SPELLING, PUNCTUATION AND GRAMMAR (S.P.G.). At Level 3 Communication these are expected to be very accurate and moderators are directed to expect very few errors. There are no allowances for poor performance at this level and, if the moderators are in any doubt, they can call for other pieces of your work for confirmation of your competence or decide that your work has not reached the required standard.

- Make very certain that you can spell all the vocabulary associated with your school/college subjects, make certain that you are familiar with paragraphs, apostrophes and commas, and use them.

- Get used to reading through your work and checking for spelling and punctuation errors. Lack of attention to detail when presenting work is very common and it lets you down. It suggests to your reader that you cannot be bothered or, worse still, that you don't know how to spell or punctuate.

ASKING FOR HELP AND SUPPORT

If S.P.G. is likely to be a big problem for you, then you do need to ask for advice and support from your teachers. Most schools/colleges offer support in a sensitive and caring way with teachers who are trained to offer you strategies for learning spelling rules and coping with punctuation. Do not rely on a spellcheck to do the work for you – you cannot take it into the final test.

REMEMBER...

Your work in the External Assessment Test and the Portfolio will be assessed on your ability to use spelling, punctuation and grammar to a very high degree of accuracy. Aim to improve them in all of your work.

Where are you now?

Self-Assessment Test

The Self-Assessment test on page 14 is to start you thinking about Key Skills and give you a feel for what Level 3 Communication is about.

Now, be honest with yourself and go through the self-assessment, ticking the most appropriate boxes. See page 15 for how to score the test.

Yes	You can always do this and have lots of evidence that you could use to demonstrate/prove your skills.
Maybe	You do some of this but as yet you are not very confident that you always do it.
No	This is something you do not feel comfortable with and you need opportunities to learn and practise.

The Self-Assessment Test is not written in terms of the Key Skills specification for Communication Level 3 – it is a range of general statements that should give you a 'feel' for what Communication is about. It should be used as an aid to start you thinking!

SKILL	Yes	Maybe	No	Score
1. DISCUSSIONS				
Can you vary your contribution to suit the situation and audience i.e. formal, informal?				
Can you keep to a line of argument or reasoning?				
Are you a good listener: can you be sensitive to other peoples ideas even if you not agree, through listening and responding?				
Can you develop ideas?				
Do you make space for others to make their contribution and offer them encouragement to make their points?				
2. MAKING PRESENTATIONS				
Do you always prepare presentations that fit their purpose, presenting a point of view in a debate or presenting findings from a piece of research?				
Can you ensure that your vocabulary and style meet the needs of your topic and your audience?				
Do you use structure to clarify and sequence your main points?				
Do you use examples to help illustrate your point, or do you use diagrams or charts or other visual aids to help engage your audience?				
3. READING AND SYNTHESISING INFORMATION				
Can you skim read, use indexes and chapter headings to identify whether a text is going to be useful to you?				
Do you scan to find specific material that you require?				
Can you use reference sources to help you understand complex concepts in texts and images?				
Do you know when to ask others for help/clarification?				
Do you know the difference between fact and opinion; can you recognise bias in writing – including your own?				
When you have obtained information, can you bring it together in your own words in a structured and coherent form, for example an essay or a report, and offer up your own interpretation?				
4. WRITING DOCUMENTS				
Do you select the appropriate way to present your information to suit your purpose, e.g. an essay or report, with diagrams, footnotes, bibliography and so on?				
Can you select an appropriate style of writing to suit the subject and the audience: formal or informal, tone, sensitivity of the subject and so on?				
Is your work always coherent in terms of paragraphs, subheadings, linking of information, highlighting, italics and so on?				
Can you proof read and redraft your work, taking into consideration the accuracy of your spelling, punctuation and grammar, so that meaning is clear? (You would not be penalised for one or two errors if you do not make the same errors in other documents.)				
TOTAL				

How to score your Self-Assessment Test

Score as follows:

2 marks for every 'YES' you ticked

1 mark for every 'MAYBE' you ticked

0 marks if you ticked 'NO'

What your score should tell you

This assessment is just a quick way of showing you where your strengths and weaknesses are. YOU CANNOT FAIL THIS ASSESSMENT!

If you scored:

38 or 0	You are far too optimistic or pessimistic. Do the assessment again!
25 +	This is a more realistic result. What this would suggest is that you already have some strengths to build on but you need practice in a range of skills in order to get to the right level. This book offers opportunities for practice and offers suggestions for further improvement. You should be able to achieve Level 3 with careful planning.
Below 25	If you think that you have answered accurately then you need to think very carefully about how you are going to develop your skills to an appropriate level. The exercises in this book will help but it might also be useful to investigate what support and help you can access at school or college. It may be that you have always felt that you lack confidence in some areas and it is now a good time to get to grips with this before going on to HE.

At this point you are either feeling incredibly smug or very depressed! Do not worry – as stated above, assessments are really only to tell you what you probably already know or suspect. If you have gained grades A*- C in your GCSE English you should recognise that you are using many or all of the skills of Level 2 Key Skills already. The one proviso is that you **must** be accurate and consistent with your spelling, punctuation and grammar – without a dictionary or spellcheck. So you may have many of the skills already in place but need appropriate work and practice to bring them up to Level 3.

So remember, this assessment gives some idea of your **attainment** but does not assess your **potential**, which, as far as this book is concerned, is much more important. This is exactly the same principle that your teachers use in selecting you for A/S, A Level or Vocational A Level study. They know how you performed in GCSEs and they assess that you have the potential to achieve your higher level qualifications. The main point is that you now have some idea of what you can do and know, and what you need to do and know. **You** have the job of bridging this gap.

DIAGNOSTIC TESTING

Many schools and colleges have diagnostic tests, which you can sit to identify your existing level of Key Skills and to identify those skills that need development and practice. You should ask your tutors for advice.

Go back to the Self-Assessment Test on page 14 and remind yourself which skills you need to acquire and develop.

Key Skills in your studies

The intention of Curriculum 2000 is to offer you a broad base for your studies while developing a range of skills to help you progress to higher level study and the world of employment. You should consider your other qualifications carefully, with the help of your tutors if necessary, and identify where the Key Skills occur in these qualifications. This is the **ideal** way to approach Key Skills, by generating evidence within your wider studies. **Integration** will make Key Skills more relevant and manageable.

● It will be useful for you to have the opportunity to look at the specifications laid down by the Awarding Body for your main subjects of study, that is the A/S, A Level or GNVQ that forms the major focus of your work.

● Ask your teachers or the school librarian. If you have difficulties, these specifications can all be found on the Internet. It has never been easier for you to go straight to the information yourself. (You can find website addresses at the end of this book.)

● **All** the specifications for your other qualifications will have some signposting and guidance on the Key Skills you are developing while studying for these other qualifications. Make the most of these opportunities, as they will present themselves naturally as part of your studies.

● Go through these specifications and try to identify where you will have the opportunity to generate Key Skills evidence. If you are familiar with the other Key Skills you are working towards, you can jot down development/evidence opportunities for them as well.

● Many pieces of work that you undertake in other subjects can be extended/developed to meet the requirements of Key Skills evidence.

● Planning in this way will make it easier for you to meet all the evidence requirements and build your portfolio(s).

PROXY QUALIFICATIONS

Some qualifications, which you may already have achieved or be working towards, give exemption from parts of some Key Skills. There is a list of these in Appendix D (page 69). (This was accurate as of June 2000.)

If you think you may be entitled to any exemption, get your tutor to check for you.

KEY POINT

They are **your** Key Skills and as a Level 3 candidate the awarding bodies consider that **you should be very active in developing your skills**. You are not a passive recipient of knowledge. You should also apply this to your learning strategies for your other subjects.

Some ideas for practice and development

To support you in your External Assessment and to allow you to produce a portfolio of the correct quality, you need lots of opportunities to develop all the following skill areas:

★ **Taking part in discussions**
★ **Making presentations**
★ **Reading and synthesising information**
★ **Writing documents**

REMEMBER...

Opportunities for practice may **not** always be school/college based.

● Do you have a part-time job?

● Do you take part in sports or have a hobby?

● Think about the communicating you do in these settings. Try to jot down a few instances.

● Be positive about the skills that you are using already.

Taking part in discussions

(This element of Communication will be assessed as a part of your Portfolio Part B – see Unit Specification 3.1a, page 63)

What is a discussion?

In Key Skills terms, a discussion can be anything from a one-to-one conversation with a colleague or tutor at Level 1 up to a rather more formal and structured debate or meeting at Level 3.

From the skills and evidence requirements outlined in the Unit Specification, it is clear that at Level 3 there is an expectation that the discussion involves COMPLEX and often sensitive issues and that you are prepared to handle these. Examples of such issues could include race, religion, gender and politics.

Language

● Your language should be appropriate for the situation; you should not use slang and must remember to be polite, even if the discussion develops into a heated debate!

● Listen to what others are saying and decode their language. Are they really saying what they think?

● Try to avoid using emotive language. Instead, try reasoned ideas.

Body language

● Looking around your group will give you a good idea of how people are feeling and how they are responding to your contributions.

● People 'speak' with their bodies as well as their mouths; do their facial expressions agree with the words they are saying?

● Are they folding their arms to defend themselves from your comments? Are they avoiding eye contact?

Tone

● You may not agree with everything that is being said but stay calm and do not be scathing or sarcastic about other people's contributions. In the future, you will find that it pays to value the contributions of everyone.

Style

- The style of the discussion, and to some extent your language, will be determined by the subject of your discussion.

- Is the discussion set up as a formal meeting with an agenda and a chairperson, are minutes being taken or is it perhaps a more informal opportunity to 'bounce' around some ideas? You must know beforehand or you can easily fall into the trap of being unprepared.

Keeping to the point

- When you have something to say, keep to the point. Many meetings or discussions drag on because people meander off the subject.

- If you are chairing or leading a discussion, it is important to keep people to the point and focused. You can be polite and remind them that time is short and you must move the discussion on – much more polite than looking at your watch!

- One tip is to set a timed agenda, limit the meeting and tell participants what decisions they have to achieve.

- Most meetings can be approached in this way. Open-ended meetings and discussion merely expand to fill the time available.

Keeping notes

- Even if formal minutes are kept of your discussion, you can also make notes for your Key Skills folder. You can do this during or immediately after the discussion. This will remind you of your role in the discussion, what you agreed to do and it can act as supporting evidence if you use this particular discussion as Key Skills evidence. It could act as evidence for Working With Others.

- You might like to reflect on your own performance and make some notes on this. If you have someone in your group with whom you feel comfortable, you could swap notes and help each other with some constructive criticism and mutual support. Could you use this for Improving Own Learning and Performance?

- Keeping notes is not essential for your Key Skills Communication portfolio but they can be good to look back on, to jog your memory and can be good practice for other situations. They could provide evidence for other Key Skills.

MAKING CONNECTIONS

By getting to know the Unit Specifications for all of your Key Skills you can start to make connections. Pieces of work that you use for evidence in one Key Skill may also cover some of the evidence requirements of another Key Skill.

Evidence you create for the section above may also cover:

WWO	3.1	3.2	3.3
LP	3.1		
IT	3.1		

★ See page 8 for further information on the wider Key Skills.
  Visit www.qca.org.uk for detailed Unit Specifications.

Making presentations

(This element of Communication will be assessed as part of your Portfolio Part B – see Unit Specification 3.1b, page 63)

What is a presentation?

A presentation is normally used as a way of presenting information or findings to a group of people in a structured way. The audience may be just a few people with whom you are familiar, but could be a more formal affair, where you speak to a large number of people in a lecture theatre or auditorium. Key Skills can prepare you for both situations, however daunting they may appear.

GCSE English oral assessment

Many students will already have 'done' presentations as a part of their oral assessment in their English GCSE. Teachers may have expected this skill from you in other subjects. There is absolutely no doubt that standing up in front of that sea of faces for the first time can be a daunting experience. Everyone has some nerves when facing a group of people and sharing with them your ideas, findings or instructions. It does get easier with practice and speaking in front of people is a vital skill for most employment routes.

Making sure of your brief

Make certain that before you begin you have all the information you need.

- What are you required to do?
- When do you have to do it?
- Who will be the audience?
- How long will you have to speak?
- Are you being assessed?
- Are you expected to produce handouts/visual aids beforehand?
- Can you choose how to set out the room?
- Are there any specific things that you need, e.g. OHP, white-boards etc.?

Preparation

It may only be a presentation in front of your tutor group, and here the word 'only' can be misleading, but it is vitally important that you prepare. By asking the above questions you can take CONTROL.

Planning and structure

- You can approach a presentation in the same way as you would an essay.
- You have to be sure of your topics and then go away and do your research.
- You need to read widely and, at sixth form and Key Skills Level 3 standard, you should be reading from a wide variety of often complicated and unfamiliar texts.
- Don't forget the requirement for COMPLEX documents in both your reading and writing.
- The quality and level of the books and other resources you use to research your presentation will, to a large extent, define its level.

THE INGREDIENTS OF A SUCCESSFUL PRESENTATION

All successful presentations have:

1) **A strong and concise introduction where you outline to your audience what it is that you are going to tell them.**

2) **The body of your presentation, which can be broken into the verbal equivalent of paragraphs: clear and logically connected 'chunks', where you give information and explanations.**

3) **A conclusion where you bring the information together, by recapping on your points and coming to some resolution.**

- A presentation will often be designed as an 'argument' where you are expected to bring together a range of other people's views, ideas or theories.

- When you get to the end, make sure that you finish by coming down on one side or the other of the argument. Do not sit on the fence – it appears 'wishy-washy' and as if you cannot make a decision based on the evidence.

- It does not matter what you conclude as long as you have a good and well-reasoned argument to back you up.

- Your style and the degree of formality will depend on your subject and audience. The important thing is to fulfil the requirements of the Unit Specification.

- Be prepared to answer any questions afterwards and, if you don't know the answer, don't be afraid to say so. Simply answer, 'I'm not sure of that but I'll certainly try to find out'. You don't have to know everything!

Coping with nerves

- There is no magic formula for coping with nerves when giving a presentation.

- Try some deep breaths in and out and be aware of tension in your body. It is difficult to be tense if your shoulders and hands are relaxed so try a few shrugs and finger waggling – preferably in a discrete way.

- In general, the best advice is, as discussed above, to be prepared. It is also worth choosing a topic, if possible, that no one else has chosen. In this way you can normally be assured of being an 'expert' on the subject in front of an eager audience.

- Another tip is to make eye contact with members of your audience, even if you are only with fellow students in a seminar room. Make eye contact with your teacher. He or she will invariably smile back to encourage you and that always helps. In general, people will be supportive of your efforts because, after all, they will probably be next in the 'hot seat'.

TIP

> Presentations form a huge part of teaching at sixth form and college level and are used for many assessments on undergraduate programmes. Developing these skills and gaining confidence in speaking in front of others will give you an excellent preparation for higher level study and for interviews and the world of work.

Body language

- Try to appear positive and confident even if you are 'wilting' inside. It is always far better if you deliver your presentation standing up, even if you have the choice to remain seated. Your extra height over those seated gives you a psychological advantage.

- Be aware of any idiosyncratic gestures that you may have and try to control them. Waving your hands around or nodding all the time can be very distracting to your audience. Videoing yourself can give you useful feedback on this.

- Above all, smile, engage others with eye contact and be relaxed. If you appear to be enjoying what you are saying your audience will respond. You may feel comfortable enough with a friend or parent to practise at home or at least have a go in front of the mirror. Imagine yourself in the audience – would this presentation interest you?

Tone and style

- Without knowing the subject and audience it is often difficult to advise on style and tone. Only you will know what is expected of you.

- The subject of your presentation will determine whether you can inject any humour into your delivery. The Key Skills specification requires that you have an 'appropriate' tone and style, so this is the criterion you should bear in mind. Do not, however, confuse humour with content. Even though you may want to amuse your audience, this should not be at the expense of the rigour of your argument.

- You will know if the occasion is formal, in which case your style and tone should match. Never be sarcastic or scathing. Be respectful of other people's arguments and feelings. Do not swear or use slang, unless it is used in a 'technical' way to illustrate a particular point.

- Formal does not have to mean pompous: it really suggests that you know the content and context of your presentation and are prepared to deliver it in a professional manner.

- Never read your presentation from a script. You will lose your place and panic and, worse still, your audience will die of boredom. Use prompt cards – one or two small cards with your key points written on them. If you use OHP transparencies, these can be your prompts.

- As for any performance, rehearsal is essential. Tone and style complement your body language. You can practise in front of the mirror, or using a tape recorder or a video recorder. It can be horrifying to see yourself as others do – but it can be worthwhile if your presentation technique improves.

TIP
> **Most schools/colleges have staff who are trained in the media, presentation skills or the performing arts. Try asking for some tips and training.**

Visual aids and handouts

- It is perhaps best not to give the audience a copy of your handouts before you begin. They will not be able to resist reading them while you are speaking, and they will not listen to you.

- If you do intend to give out an outline of your talk, tell the audience that they do not need to make notes.

- If you are going to use any electrical equipment make sure that **it works** and **you know how to use it**.

- If you need any equipment, make sure that you let your teacher know in good time; the same goes for any photocopying that you may want done.

- If you are trying to explain anything that is essentially visual, you should use photocopies or an OHP or both. It can be very confusing if you are talking about a diagram or a picture and your audience cannot share the IMAGE.

- Do not forget that being able to use appropriate images to support a point or argument is a Communication skill that will be assessed.

AND THEN...

There is nothing quite like a presentation that has gone well. You were well prepared, the audience was supportive and enjoyed your remarks and, above all, your teacher thought you did well. The adrenaline rush stays with you for hours! After all that you wonder what you were worried about.

MAKING CONNECTIONS

> **By getting to know the Unit Specifications for all of your Key Skills you can start to make connections. Pieces of work that you use for evidence in one Key Skill may also cover some of the evidence requirements of another Key Skill.**
>
> **Evidence you create for the section above may also cover:**
>
> | PS | 3.1 | 3.2 | |
> |----|-----|-----|-----|
> | LP | 3.1 | 3.2 | 3.3 |
> | IT | 3.1 | 3.2 | 3.3 |
>
> ★ See page 8 for further information on the wider Key Skills.
>   Visit www.qca.org.uk for detailed Unit Specifications.

Reading and synthesising information

(See Unit Specification 3.2, page 63)

How do you read?

You may think this is a very silly question, but think about it: at home reading a thriller or novel do you read the same way as you do in school/college when confronted with a textbook?

No, we all read in different ways in different situations. It depends on what we are expected to get out of our reading.

Reading for a purpose

Although it is often unconscious, we generally do know the purpose of our reading.

● With a novel the purpose is to quickly grasp the plot and follow the storyline in order to reach the conclusion. The storyline itself usually helps with our understanding and, although it may describe contexts and situations that we have not experienced, there are cultural assumptions that we all share, which allow us to make 'sense' of the story.

● When we read a textbook or a non-fiction work, we have another purpose in mind. Usually this is to find out information in terms of facts, arguments or data. You need to be able to select and read material that contains the information you require.

● This is a specialised form of reading and one that you have to come to terms with as you progress up the ladder of education. Often, there are concepts and vocabulary that are new and challenging and you need time 'to get your head around' the subject. For example, if you have started on a course for Psychology, Sociology or Economics A/S Level you will be coming across theories and models of the world and the behaviour of people that seem very complex and which you may not have encountered before.

● Every academic discipline has its own vocabulary and at first you may feel excluded. Don't worry about this – it is normal when moving on to new subjects and new qualifications. You will soon become familiar with the new vocabulary.

● You must ensure that you identify accurately and compare the lines of reasoning, the writer's argument, and the main points from texts and images. This key information then has to be synthesised, brought together, in a form relevant to your purpose.

Skimming and scanning

There is no doubt whatsoever that a good reading speed is an advantage to your studies, but focusing your reading and improving your study techniques are also important.

● So many students want to read and make notes at the same time, erroneously believing that this will save them time. It doesn't.

● If you work in this way you will simply re-write the whole text in your own words. Some students end up creating notes that are longer than the original text! Why? Because they have not read, understood and extracted the key points.

TIPS ON TAKING NOTES

1) Read through the text without worrying about writing. Do you understand what the text is about? If not, do you need further supplementary reading to help you?
2) Take a short break – a couple of minutes is adequate – and then come back to the text. Do you still remember the main points? If not read it carefully again.
3) When you are happy that you understand the text, go through with a highlighter pen and mark the main points made by the writer.
4) Now is the time to write. Make notes that will make sense to you next week, next month or even next year.

Making notes that mean something

This may sound obvious but how many times have you opened your notes to revise and realised that you have not got a clue what you were thinking at the time?

- Don't forget that most texts have a structure: the writer has done what you are advised to do.
- There should be an introduction, paragraphs making specific points and a conclusion.
- Think of making notes as reversing the process of essay planning: you are going backwards from the essay to the plan, picking the meat off the skeleton.

There are two types of notes that students tend to use. Which one, if any, you use will be down to personal preference.

Linear notes

<u>Heading</u>

<u>Subheading</u>

- point 1
- point 2
- point 3 etc.

Mind mapping

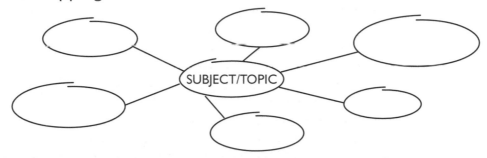

SUBJECT/TOPIC

- **Whenever possible, go back to your notes within a few days and see if they make sense.**
- **Can you remember why you wrote them?**
- **If necessary, make small additions to help make your understanding clearer.**

To sum up:

★ **Think** before you write – why are you making these notes?

★ Be **succinct.**

★ **Use** a style of note-taking that works for you

★ **Review** your notes after a few days and add/change them if needed.

★ **Learn** from your note-taking disasters.

Bias, fact and opinion

- When you read other people's work, you are sometimes aware that they have a point of view to put forward. They might tell you from the outset that they have a particular interest in proving a point or they may have a political allegiance, for example, that will influence the style and content of their writing. This is fine, as it forewarns you to be aware of bias and emotive language.

- More problematic are accounts that purport to be neutral and factual but are, in fact, loaded with opinion and bias. This is often the situation with newspaper accounts, whether they are broadsheets or tabloids. Newspapers are not publicly owned – they have an owner who often wants his press to reflect and support his political opinions, so for example *The Daily Telegraph* and *The Daily Mail* are known to support the Conservative cause and *The Guardian* supports Labour. In this way, the readership can buy the paper that is most likely to confirm and reinforce their own opinions.

- When students are confronted with the press it is often difficult for them to identify news, fact and opinion within a particular newspaper. Papers contain so much 'old' news, compared to satellite television, terrestrial television, radio and the Internet, that they do tend to contain a great deal of opinion and comment. So beware!

- Whenever you read anything, ask yourself where the evidence comes from for that writer to make that statement. Ask the following:

   Who has written the text, what do you know about them?

   What have they written: is it an article, feature, editorial etc.?

   Why has the piece been written: to inform, to support a political stance etc.?

- You must also be careful in your writing that you are not guilty of bias. Try to back up everything that you say with evidence from your research.

- This does not mean that you cannot have an opinion but it must be an opinion based on evidence.

- In an essay or report your reader must be able to see where you have found your material and how it has led you to form your conclusion (opinion).

- Once you are aware of the existence of bias and opinion presented as fact, you will be more sensitive and careful in your reading of texts.

> The requirements of the Communication Unit Specification at Level 3 mean that you must go beyond SUMMARY. You must be assessing facts, opinions and ideas and bringing them together, synthesising, to present your own interpretation. Make sure that this is what you are doing.

Keeping your material in order

Think seriously about getting organised. This may not be a problem for you but here are a few tips anyway.

- Get yourself some stationery: ring binders, plastic wallets, magazine holders.
- Highlighter pens and correction fluid are invaluable.
- Assign a colour for each subject so you can find work at a glance.
- Sort out any work that can be archived and file it at home. Don't continue to carry it around with you every day – it will get dog-eared or you will lose it. Don't hoard.
- Remember some of this work will be needed in 12 to 18 months' time. Review your notes on a regular basis and revision will never be from 'scratch'.

TIP

> As with anything else you do as a student, **don't** be tempted to cut corners – it does not pay. Spending time setting up a system to file and store your work will save time in the future when you want to find work for revision or to put in your Key Skills portfolio.

By getting to know the Unit Specifications for all of your Key Skills you can start to make connections. Pieces of work that you use for evidence in one Key Skill may also cover some of the evidence requirements of another Key Skill.

Evidence you create for the section above may also cover:

LP	3.2	3.3
IT	3.1	3.2

★ See page 8 for further information on the wider Key Skills.
Visit www.qca.org.uk for detailed Unit Specifications.

EXERCISE

On the next few pages there are three articles for you to use for note-taking practice.

They are not as EXTENDED as the documents you will be expected to use for evidence at Level 3 but they will give you an idea of how to start making your notes more efficiently and effectively.

1) **Violence against airline crew**

2) **The safety of car airbags** (also uses IMAGES)

3) **Paying privately for surgery** (includes a table)

Read each article and make notes. You can make linear notes or draw a mindmap (see page 23), or you can use another note-taking style with which you feel comfortable.

When you have worked through these articles, turn to the answers in Chapter 7 and see how your notes compare.

Airlines conceal attacks on crew

AIR rage incidents are five times more common than previously revealed, according to figures in an internal British Airways report, *write Tom Robbins and David Leppard.*

The airline's official statistics show only 122 "air rage" incidents in the year up to March 1999. However, the document obtained by The Sunday Times revealed that cabin crew are having to cope with more than 644 incidents of physical and verbal abuse annually.

In the first six months of 1999, 13 passengers were handcuffed on BA flights and four flights were diverted because of disruptive passengers. In one case a 29-year-old British electrician attacked two passengers and punched through the inner pane of a window on a flight to Bangkok.

The man, who had drunk three double whiskies and taken Valium, also tried to eat a young woman's headphones after grabbing them when she rebuffed his advances. Four cabin crew and a soldier fought him to the floor and handcuffed him while the plane was diverted to Delhi.

The figures are contained in a report by the British Airways cabin crew confidential safety reporting team, a unit set up to allow crew to report safety concerns and incidents privately, rather than make official statements.

Because crew can report safety incidents without fear of becoming involved in any follow-up action or court proceedings, the system is believed to give a more accurate picture of the problem.

Last month the Civil Aviation Authority announced the results of the government's first survey of air rage cases, which found 800 incidents in seven months on all British aircraft — one incident per 870 flights. The BA figures show cabin crew exposed to abusive passengers on one in 440 flights.

Dave Kelly, industrial relations officer for Cabin Crew 89, 'the crews' union, said the problem was being made worse by airports putting in more facilities where passengers could drink while waiting for their planes.

BA cabin crew are insured against air rage attacks and the company offers counselling to staff who are victims. Crew are also trained in how to calm aggressive passengers and in the use of handcuffs.

BA said the official statistics covered only the most serious cases, but added: "We take all these incidents very seriously and have been at the forefront in developing initiatives to combat the problem."

Last year the government responded to growing concern over air rage attacks by making it an offence to threaten or abuse aircraft crew. Offenders face up to two years in prison and a £5,000 fine.

Airbag kills driver in 19mph crash

Roger Dobson

DETAILS of the first death in Britain directly caused by a car airbag were revealed last week.

The victim, a 47-year-old woman from Merseyside, died when the bag blasted into her head, breaking her skull and causing brain damage. Her car was travelling at only 19 miles an hour.

Doctors said yesterday that her injuries were more like those suffered by someone falling from a building and landing on their head than a seat-belted victim of a low-speed car crash.

The woman was killed when her Rover collided with another vehicle. The driver of the other car, an Opel, which did not have an airbag, walked away with only a cut lip.

Doctors are now warning drivers and front-seat passengers that they must sit at least 10in from the airbag covers to avoid similar accidents.

The concerns raised by the woman's death come as a growing number of manufacturers include airbags as standard in British cars.

Airbag-related injuries are already a problem in America, where more than 70% of vehicles are fitted with the devices. According to the US National Highways Traffic Safety Administration, 145 people have died as a result of airbag impact, including 84 children, 18 of whom were infants in rear-facing child seats. A spokesman said: "The one fact that is common to all who died is not their height, weight, sex or age, but the fact that they were too close to the airbag when it started to deploy."

British airbags are primarily designed to stop a driver wearing a seatbelt from coming into contact with the steering wheel, whereas American airbags are designed to protect unbelted passengers. Seatbelts are not mandatory in all states.

The British airbags, at around 40 litres in size, are smaller than the American ones, which are about 70 litres. Although the British bags inflate with much less force, inflation takes the same time: 50 milliseconds.

Details of the death of the woman from Merseyside are reported by doctors in the current issue of the British Journal of Accident and Emergency Medicine.

"It is the first fatality in Britain directly attributable to an airbag," said Patrick Nee, a consultant in accident and emergency medicine at Whiston hospital, Merseyside, one of a team of four authors of the report. Although the woman was tall — 5ft 7ins — Nee said "it was her habit to sit quite close to the steering wheel, and we believe she probably died because she was sitting too near".

It has been known for some time that airbags can cause minor injuries, including bruises and abrasions to the face and neck, and chest injuries. They can also cause eye injuries, especially if the victim is wearing glasses.

Doctors believe the woman came into contact with the bag as it was inflating. It hit her with enough force to cause a huge fracture at the base of her skull.

"The bag needs to be fully deployed before you hit it. There is a detonation charge in the bag which produces gas that expands it very rapidly," said Nee. "The idea is that the fully deployed airbag is there to meet you as you travel forward with the deceleration of impact, and you bounce off it. You don't want to be hitting it when it is still expanding."

Concerns about the accident were raised because the cars were going slowly, yet the woman's injuries were so severe. "It was a relatively modest crash from which the other driver walked away," said Nee. "Her injuries alerted us to the possibility that this was no ordinary head injury. It was a ring fracture of the skull, which means a major force was applied."

In their report, the doctors warn that more airbag injuries are likely as an increasing proportion of cars have them fitted. They also advise people who are shorter than average to contact the manufacturers and to consider disabling the airbags.

A spokesman for the Society of Motor Manufacturers and Traders disagreed: "There should be no consideration of disconnecting airbags. It would be irresponsible to interfere in that way with something that has had such a huge role in reducing deaths."

An AA spokesman said: "Most people hurt by the bags would have been injured much more severely had they hit the steering wheel. It is very much a freak accident."

Manufacturers are now designing "smart" airbags, which adjust according to the speed of the accident and the passenger's weight and position. They are expected to be fitted in some cars soon.

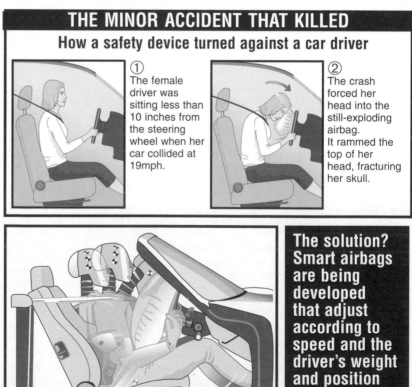

THE MINOR ACCIDENT THAT KILLED
How a safety device turned against a car driver

① The female driver was sitting less than 10 inches from the steering wheel when her car collided at 19mph.

② The crash forced her head into the still-exploding airbag. It rammed the top of her head, fracturing her skull.

The solution? Smart airbags are being developed that adjust according to speed and the driver's weight and position

Best ways to pay for your operations

GORDON BROWN'S health giveaway announced in the budget has been welcomed, but for many people it will be too late. Thousands of patients are already on waiting lists and thousands more will find themselves in need of urgent care before his billions kick in.

The frustration of the waiting-list scandal and the rising cost of medical insurance is prompting more and more people to simply pay for operations themselves.

In 1999, 160,000 people paid for surgery in private hospitals — about 17% of the private medical market. An advantage of paying yourself over insurance is that there are no policy exclusions to catch you out.

So what does private medical treatment cost? Paying your way clearly requires an up-front lump sum, though it may not be as high as you expect. Table 1 shows the typical range of costs for the main operations carried out by private hospitals.

The main hospitals do not vary a great deal in their estimates, although a case that is very straightforward, or very complicated, might fall well outside the limits in our tables.

Included is Surgicare (0800 622222), a company specialising in only four types of surgery: cataracts, hernias, varicose veins and certain cosmetic procedures. Most work is done on a day-case basis, so patients do not normally stay overnight. They can expect to be treated within two to six weeks of referral.

Paying your own way is not a panacea. Some operations are costly — perhaps beyond the scope of savings or a loan. A heart bypass operation, for example, could cost £12,500, says Bupa.

In response to demand from patients wanting to pay for operations private hospitals offer a range of finance arrangements.

Fixed-price treatment

All the main private-hospital chains now offer this. Patients are given a fixed cost tailored to their case after an initial assessment by a consultant. Unforeseen extras will normally be included. Payment can be made by credit card and must be made in advance.

Finance arrangement

Bupa, Community Hospitals and Nuffield Hospitals all offer unsecured medical loans, with rates of up to 15.9%. Nuffield offers interest-free credit on loans repaid within 12 months.

BMI group has its own credit card that offers six months' interest-free credit. The maximum credit limit is £5,000, although this is likely to be increased. The rate is 15.5%.

On a £5,000 loan over three years in the non-specialist market you can pay from £160.11 a month without credit-protection insurance (Lombard Direct 0800 215000). With insurance, American Express Bank (0808 1002265) is among the cheapest at £181.40.

The medical insurance industry started to fight the tide of self-pay this week as Standard Life launched Choices, which has three elements. The first is a high-excess insurance policy to cover people prepared to pay their way but who want protection against big bills. It pays out if a claim comes to more than the chosen excess amount of £1,000, £2,500 or £5,000.

Monthly premiums for a man aged 50 are £37.01, £23.77 or £16. A family of four where the oldest parent is 45 would pay £51.88, £29.96 or £18.70. They would pay about £100 a month for a standard medical policy.

Choices also offers a treatment information service to help find surgery at reasonable cost; and an investment option where Standard Life's range of savings products can be used to build up a medical emergency fund. WPA's internet product xshealth (www.xshelth.co.uk) claims to be the first to combine insurance with self-pay. Given its low cost, it could be used to fill a gap for a few years while you build up a savings fund.

There is a further option. Humphrey Nicholls, Surgicare's managing director, says: "The government has created a wonderful vehicle for self-pay through Isas." Putting money into your own savings certainly seems more attractive than paying it in premiums to a medical insurer that gives no benefits if you do not claim.

Table 1

COST OF THE MOST COMMON OPERATIONS

	Cataract (one eye)	Varicose veins	Hernia	Hip replacement
Bupa	£1,800-2400	£1,000-1500	£1,000-1,500	£5,000-7,800
Nuffield	£1,950-2600	£1,300-1,425	£1,350-1,700	£5,800-7,500
Surgicare	£1,300	£975	£1,050	

Table 2

THE COST OF CREDIT

Medical loans	Interest free period	APR%	Age limits	Min/Max amount of loan	Deposit	Cost per month without insurance[1]
Community Hospitals Group 08453010088	none	14.9	22-75	£1,000-£10,000	10%	£168.65
Bupa 08456008822	none	14.9	18-80	£1,000-£10,000	10%	£168.65
Nuffield 0800688699	1 year	15.9	18-79	£500-£10,000	10%	£172.95[2]
Credit card BMI Card 08456008822	6 months	15.5	min 18	no min Max £5,000	–	

[1]Figure for £5,000 borrowed over three year, excluding any deposits. [2]does not include any interest–free payments

Writing documents

(See Unit Specification 3.3, page 63)

For the majority of you, the most common documents you will be required to produce will be essays and reports. If you have a look at the specification for Communication Level 3, you will see that for your evidence you must produce two different types of document. The following pages will give you some tips on how to plan and produce an essay and a report. Remember, the emphasis is on quality. Good preparation and organisation will improve the quality of your work. There are also some tips on memos and formal letters. Your portfolio of evidence could include an example of one of these less academic types of writing as one of the two documents required. At Level 3 **you** must choose the most appropriate written format for your evidence. You should also be prepared to justify your choice.

Let the medium fit the message

- It is important that the form of written communication you use does fit the message and your purpose. If your principal wants to let colleagues know about a change in the college calendar he/she will not write an essay for them – a simple memo outlining the main details will be sufficient. If he/she wants to present information to heads of department in response to a request for details he/she might write a report outlining the main points and making recommendations.

- The same memo can be sent to many people – it is impersonal.

- A letter is usually personal and the contents are directed specifically at the recipient.

- Some written documents are enhanced by charts, diagrams or pictures in order to illustrate and clarify meaning. You should be aware of when this is the case, as the Unit Specification requires the use of an IMAGE in at least one piece of evidence for C3.3. (IMAGES can include charts, diagrams, sketches etc.)

Style

- You should always be aware of your audience and ensure that your tone and vocabulary are appropriate. Don't use slang. In essays it is generally not considered 'good' style to use contractions: won't, don't, didn't etc.

- Be careful with words that may be considered emotive or where you could be accused of bias or making value judgements.

- At Level 3, most of your writing is going to be quite formal and academic: after all you are working towards A/S, A Level and Vocational A Level qualifications. So, don't forget the word COMPLEX, which you came across earlier in this book: you are expected to be able to deal with and express COMPLEX subjects and use any associated vocabulary.

- Organising your material in an appropriate way is also important and will be discussed over the next few pages.

Redrafting and proof reading

- Students who produce their work using IT have their work on disk and when they are not happy with their essay, report etc. they can move paragraphs about, edit and redraft on screen.

- This tends not to happen when someone has a handwritten 2000-word essay. (Remember the Key Skills definition of EXTENDED is three sides.) They simply do not want the chore of rewriting.

- If you can get used to word processing your work, and if your teachers allow it, it can save you time. (With careful planning it may also be used as Key Skills IT evidence.)

- Some people find it difficult to proof read from a PC monitor, so print out a hard copy.
- Whether printed or handwritten, do remember the stringent requirements of Key Skills for accurate spelling, punctuation and grammar. If in doubt, let someone else have a look through your work before you hand it in.
- Above all, if you get work back from your teachers commenting on any of these three, **do something about it!** You will not gain your Level 3 in Communication, no matter how brilliant your ideas and content, if you fall down on spelling, punctuation and grammar. You must satisfy all of the evidence components and you cannot afford to disregard this.

Now we will have a look at the documents you are most likely to produce...

How to write an essay

You will have done this many times but do you actually follow any kind of plan or strategy? You may choose to produce an essay as the EXTENDED document for component 3.3 of your portfolio.

The title

- What is the question asking? If you don't know, you won't know what to read or how to answer the question.
- Underline key words.
- If you still don't understand, ask friends or your tutor.

Brainstorming/deciding on an outline

- Get a blank piece of paper and write the essay title in the middle.
- Around this title, brainstorm topics you think may be included, using single words or phrases. You might cluster some of them together like in the mind maps earlier on.
- Now try to order your points so that you have a structure to follow. What do you already know? What do you need to find out?
- Don't simply use everything you know about the subject. This is a very common fault with students. Be selective, do further reading and keep looking back to make sure that you are answering the question or addressing the title. Keep this piece of paper in a safe place!

Collecting material for your essay

- Check your class notes/handouts for any useful material.
- Has your teacher given you a reading list?
- Can you use your library catalogue? Is it computerised?
- Don't forget information can come from journals, magazines, CD ROMs, the Internet and many other sources besides books.
- **Always** keep a note of where you found your information: title, author, publisher, date of publication and page numbers.
- When you are researching, use this checklist before diving straight into the book or article:

  Main title

  Look at the index

  Chapter headings

  Scan the introduction

Scan the conclusion

Only then... read the relevant bits

- Keep referring back to your title to make sure you don't wander off the question.

Planning your essay

- After you have completed your reading/research, go back to your original piece of paper and add the notes that you have made.
- You can now start to develop and link points on your plan and you will see a structure developing.
- Some people like to write out each key point on a separate sheet, together with any supporting material. You can order the points logically.

All of the above has been written as if you are working on paper. Of course, all of it can be done equally well on screen on your PC.

The first draft

- Different teachers expect different styles when you write for them. Generally, academic essays are written in the third person – 'this essay will demonstrate', 'thus it can be seen…' etc. Ask your teachers if this is what they want. They may accept the use of 'I' – 'In this essay I will…' – but check first. The ability to adapt your style is an important communication skill.

All essays should have:

Introduction

(You can write this after you have prepared the main body of your essay.)
This is normally around a paragraph long and should not exceed 10% of your total words. It says what you are going to do in your essay and how you will go about this. The introduction should define any vocabulary, key words or phrases. It should also show how your content relates to the title.

Main body

This is the bulk of your essay, where you answer the question. You can now take the points from your plan and write about them using the evidence you have researched. It may be appropriate to use a paragraph for each main point you wish to make. Try to avoid over-long paragraphs and do not fall into the trap of plagiarism – you must reference other people's ideas and words. That is why it is important to keep this information as you do your reading.

Conclusion

Like the introduction, this should ideally be a paragraph long and restricted to 10% of the overall word count. This is where you must summarise the main ideas developed in the body of your work. You should also refer back to the title and show how you have answered the question. Don't use 'and so it can be seen…' if it can't! Try to use the essay as a chance to demonstrate your understanding of the topic and your ability to answer the question.

Reviewing and redrafting

Once you have written your essay, it is best to give yourself some time away from the topic. Go back to it after a few days and ask yourself the following questions:

- Have I answered the question?
- Is the content relevant and accurate?
- Have I written in a logical sequence, i.e. does the essay 'flow'?
- Can I back up all the points I have made with evidence?

- Do I acknowledge other people's ideas and have I provided a bibliography?
- Have I got a strong introduction?
- Have I got a good conclusion?

Don't forget spelling, punctuation and grammar. Look at the way you use commas, apostrophes and inverted commas, as well as your use of full stops, capital letters and the accuracy of your spelling and grammar.

Only now should you write your final draft.

EXERCISE

You are asked to discuss the following:

'The commercial benefits of genetically modified food far outweigh any health risks'

Without doing any research, jot done a few points you would need to cover and try to formulate a simple plan to work from.

Look at the example answer in Chapter 7.

Some tips on referencing and bibliographies

References show where you have found your information and ideas.

Bibliographies list the books etc. you have used in your research.

Quoting references within a text

All statements, opinions etc. taken from another writer's work should be acknowledged, whether directly quoted or summarised. There are two common ways of doing this which link with your bibliography at the end of your essay.

British Standard

Publications are numbered in the order in which they are first referred to in the text and given numbers to identify them:

For example: In a recent report, Jones (3) argues that...

Numerical references are sometimes listed at the foot of the page (this can be done easily on a PC), at the end of a chapter or at the end of the work.

Harvard System

Publications are referred to in the text by the author's name and the year of publication.

For example: In a recent report, Jones (1998) argues that...

References at the end of text

British Standard

Entries are numerical to match the numbers in the text.
1. Wood, A. Nineteenth Century Britain 1815-1914, Longman, 1982
2. Blodgett, H. Centuries of Female Days, Rutgers University Press, 1988
3. Light, A. Forever England, Routledge, 1991
4. Steedman, C. Childhood Culture and Class in Britain, Routledge, 1990

Harvard System

Entries are listed alphabetically by author's name and then date.

Blodgett, H. (1988) Centuries of Female Days, Rutgers University Press.

Light, A. (1991) Forever England, Routledge.

Steedman, C. (1990) Childhood Culture and Class in Britain, Routledge.

Wood, A. (1982) Nineteenth Century Britain 1815-1914, Longman.

Whatever system you choose, you must be consistent. Look at a few textbooks to see what reference style the author uses.

MAKING CONNECTIONS

By getting to know the Unit Specifications for all of your Key Skills you can start to make connections. Pieces of work that you use for evidence in one Key Skill may also cover some of the evidence requirements of another Key Skill.

Evidence you create for the section above may also cover:

LP	3.2
IT	3.2

★ See page 8 for further information on the wider Key Skills.
Visit www.qca.org.uk for detailed Unit Specifications.

Writing a report

Many sixth form students have not produced formal reports as a part of their studies.

A report is a document that outlines a subject or problem and gathers relevant information and facts in order to present them as fully as possible. A report can and may include judgements, conclusions and recommendations.

For these reasons, any report that you write should be:

★ succinct
★ easily understood
★ in a logical sequence
★ appropriate for its audience/reader

Before you write your report you should ask yourself:

★ Who has asked for the report?
★ Why did they ask for it?
★ What will be its purpose?
★ What does it need to include?
★ What is expected to happen as a result of the report?

You should be clear about what you are trying to achieve, otherwise your report will not be clearly focused.

Planning your report

As with essays, you can try brainstorming on a plain piece of paper, focusing on the purpose of your report. Include any key ideas or concepts and try to group this information. Look for a simple structure and try to order your ideas.

Research

What do you already know and what do you need to find out?

Record all the methods you use for your research.

Keep a note of all your sources: books, interviews, questionnaires etc.

As you progress, order your materials around the points in your plan.

Keep reviewing your work to make sure you are doing what your brief requires.

Writing your report

Your report should have the following:

- A **Title page** – this should include the title, your name and the date and, usually, the name of the person or people to whom the report will be presented.

- Sometimes people include **Acknowledgements** to people who have helped. For example, you may have written to individuals or organisations for information.

- The **Contents** – this should list the main sections and any sub-headings, together with page numbers. This is best completed after you have written your report.

- The **Introduction** – this will set the scene of your report and will outline why the report was written, what you are trying to do, your methods of investigation and the resources you used.

- The **Main Text** – this is where you detail the key findings. This should not include conclusions, opinions or recommendations. It will be the longest section of your report and should be factual.

- The **Conclusion** must connect to your terms of reference, i.e. what you set out to do. It should draw together the information in the main body as an overview and make recommendations if appropriate. Do not introduce any new 'evidence' in your conclusion.

- **Recommendations** should follow on from your conclusion and should be very specific, measurable and achievable. You can list and number your recommendations.

- Any material that is not required for the main body can go in the **Appendices**.

- You will also need to provide **References** and a **Bibliography** (see notes on referencing above).

Style and structure

- Always try to match your style to your audience. The best advice is to keep it simple and concise.

- Try not to use jargon. If you have to use specialised vocabulary, include a **Glossary**.

- Concentrate on your sentence and paragraph structure; keep them reasonably short and logically sequenced.

- Tense. Reports are written in the past tense and in the third person, i.e. 'It was observed that…'.

- You do not need to write your report in the order in which it will be finally presented. You are better to follow: main body, conclusion, recommendations, introduction, summary and title page. This does, however, require you to be organised!

Reviewing your completed report

Before handing it in you should **always** do the following:

- Check that your work is complete.

- Is it accurate?

- Check for spelling, punctuation and grammar errors.

- Check the numbering of your sections and page numbers.

Memos

The word memo is short for memorandum – a note of things to be remembered. It is a very common method of communication within business or in the everyday life of the 'office', whether that be an academic office in a college or university or the business headquarters of, say, a construction company.

The memo below has all the features required:

★ A recipient – the main person/people it is going to.

★ A CC list – a list of all the other people who need a copy.

★ A sender – who it is from.

★ A date.

★ A reference – saying what is the content of the memo.

Memos should not have:

★ More than one side of type – they are reminders and should be short.

★ A signature – you do not sign a memo.

Memorandum

To: Mary Smith
CC: All Form Reps
From: Sue Dent
Date: 11 September 2000
Re: Lockers

Would you note that there will be a short meeting in the Common Room on Friday at 12 noon to discuss the shortage of lockers.

This threatens to be a problem during the coming year and I would be pleased if you could canvass the views of your Form before this meeting.

CONFIDENTIAL

Formal letters

For much of the work for your Key Skills Communication evidence you will be working on topics that you need to research. One very common and useful way to research information is to write to organisations and companies for information.

Letters of this type should be formal letters and ideally word processed. The comments that follow assume that after drafting your letter you will word process it. This has some implications for your style.

- Most modern letters use 'open punctuation'. This means that everything is blocked, aligned to the left, and that very little punctuation is used. Ideal if you are not a brilliant typist!
- If you handwrite letters, your teachers may still expect you to indent paragraphs etc.

So remember that different approaches have different styles and are equally correct. Whichever style you adopt, you must be consistent.

Below are two letters from a student asking for information for his project.

LETTER A

```
St James High School,
Anytown,
GD4 6RT

The Manager,
Modified Foods,
Anytown,
FD5 7HJ

Dear Sir

Can you send me some information about your company? I am
doing a project at school and have to have this stuff.

Yours sincerely

Nick Cotton
```

LETTER B

```
St James High School
Anytown
GD4 6RT

Mr G Simmons
Public Relations Manager
Modified Foods
Anytown
FD5 7HJ
May 8, 2000

Dear Mr Simmons

Re: Genetically modified foods

I am a sixth form student at the above college studying for
my A/S Level General Studies. As a part of this I am required
to write an essay on the commercial implications of GM foods.

I am wondering if it would be possible for you to send me
some information about your company and its range of
products. I would also like the opportunity to come and
interview you as I have some questions to ask. You can
contact me at the school on 0456 78 42.

I look forward to receiving your reply.

Yours sincerely

Nick Cotton
```

It is not difficult to judge which letter is likely to get the best response.

Letter A

- Has no date.
- Nick hasn't bothered to find out the name of the person who can supply the information.
- Nick doesn't really explain who he is or why he needs the information.
- Dear Sir/Yours faithfully: Dear Mr Simmons/Yours sincerely – get it right.

Letter B

- Has a date.
- Names the person to whom the letter is written.
- It starts off with a reference to draw the reader straight to the point.
- Nick explains who he is and what he has to do.
- Nick explains what it is he wants.
- He ends with a pleasant and polite remark.
- He has the 'Yours sincerely' correct.

This is another occasion where a bit of planning comes in very useful.

Checklist

- The name and address of the person you are writing to.
- Your contact address, telephone, fax and/or e-mail address.
- Explain who you are and why you are writing.
- Be specific about what you expect the recipient of the letter to do. Do you want information, action etc.? Is this a requesting letter, a letter of complaint or maybe even a 'thank you'?
- Have you used the correct 'salutation', i.e. sincerely or faithfully?
- Check your style, spelling, punctuation and grammar.

TIP

> **If you are unsure about anything, get your teacher to look it over, especially if you are using school headed notepaper or the school as your return address. In this case, anything sloppy or incorrect in your letter reflects on the school as a whole and would be unacceptable as Key Skills evidence.**

This section on writing documents has covered a lot of points, which can perhaps be summarised in very few words:

★ Always **plan** your work.

★ Always **check** your work for spelling, punctuation and grammar.

★ Always **check** that your work meets its purpose.

★ If you intend to use work as Key Skills evidence, make sure it is of the very highest quality you can produce.

★ Always **ask** for advice if you are uncertain.

5 Producing your portfolio of evidence 5

What you need to do

This section is concerned with the production of your portfolio. For some this will be a new concept, while others may have done work in the past that required you to produce portfolio evidence. Don't be fooled into thinking that this is a simple 'project' where you have to put together work in a folder – the expectation is for rigorous standards to be met and it must be approached with that in mind.

The requirements for your portfolio of evidence are laid down in Part B of the Unit Specification (see page 63) and the following points should be kept in mind:

- The evidence referencing must be as laid out in the specification and all work clearly identified as to what reference you are claiming it against.
- A piece of work you produce should cover all of the requirements for that component of evidence, i.e. 3.1, 3.2 or 3.3.
- A piece of work may also cover evidence for other Key Skills.
- Thus careful planning of the work to be included in the portfolio is essential.
- The evidence covering discussion and presentations must be adequately evidenced, such as witness testimony, video evidence, background and planning notes etc.
- Action plan your work and keep a copy of this in your portfolio showing achievements and any rescheduling. This is a good reminder for you and can be used as evidence for Improving Own Learning and Performance (LP).

> On page 39 you will find a blank pro forma Evidence Tracker, which you should start to fill in as soon as possible. You will need to make extra copies, as you will find that throughout your studies you will have many opportunities to develop your Key Skills in Communication and you may choose to change the pieces of work you are putting in your portfolio of evidence.

Assessment

Your portfolio will be considered by an external moderator, appointed by your awarding body, who is there to ensure that you and your teachers are producing and assessing work worthy of Level 3 certification. Only portfolios that are complete and have been internally assessed will be accepted for external moderation. External moderators may visit your school/college or they may require samples of work through the post. They may also sit as a panel to moderate portfolios. Your teachers will have this information.

Presentation, spelling, grammar, punctuation etc. will all be taken into consideration. It is also a fact that size is not important! A 3 Kg portfolio of work, which does not fit the specification, will not pass, whereas a 1 Kg portfolio of high quality work, which addresses all the criteria, will pass. It is possible to fulfil the requirements of the specifications with as few as five or six pieces of evidence. Remember that some pieces of work will cover more than one element of evidence. If your work covers the evidence requirements, then your portfolio will achieve a 'PASS'.

Separate or integrated portfolios?

Your Key Skills evidence will ideally come from the other subjects you are studying. This makes the qualification easy to manage and reduces your workload. The question is where will you keep this evidence?

The Key Skills moderator will look at your work to see if it meets the requirements of the Key Skills specification. He/she will not judge it, for example, as a piece of biology or science work.

He/she is there solely to judge your Key Skills competence, a separate qualification. A lot will depend on how your school/college organises Key Skills.

You have two options:

1) Keep your evidence in the same place as your work for your other qualifications, for example with your English work, but keep a tracking sheet which clearly outlines for the moderator where the evidence can be found. You and your tutors must make sure that this work is accessible for the moderator.

2) Take a copy of your work, which is your evidence from your other subject, and create a separate Key Skills portfolio.

In both cases the work you are putting forward as evidence will be the same. It is really a matter of which options best suit your situation.

Evidence Tracker for Communication Level 3

You should pay special attention to the words highlighted. Some of these Key Skills terms are explained on page 10.

As you begin to gather your evidence, you can fill in your tracker sheet, making sure that you cover everything required.

Evidence component	Evidence description	Location	Date
C3.1a Contribute to a group discussion about a **COMPLEX** subject.			
C3.1b Make a presentation about a **COMPLEX** subject, using at least one **IMAGE** to illustrate complex points. IMAGE ☐			
C3.2 Read and synthesise information from two **EXTENDED** documents about a **COMPLEX** subject. Evidence 1 ☐☐☐ Evidence 2 Image in Evidence No. ☐			
C3.3 Write two different types of **EXTENDED** document about **COMPLEX** subjects. One piece of writing should be an **EXTENDED** document and include at least one **IMAGE.** Document 1 ☐☐ Document 2 1/2 Document number is extended and contains an image ☐☐			

Planning your portfolio

How you plan to gather your evidence will depend on how Key Skills is set up in your school or college. Are you aiming to get your evidence through the other qualifications that you are studying or are you producing Key Skills evidence in other sessions?

- It is important to remember that you can demonstrate your ability in Key Skills in a wide variety of settings. Indeed, the 'transferability' of Key Skills is one of their selling points.

- You must decide what you produce for your Key Skills evidence and how you do it, but if you decide to use work from other qualifications it can mean less work for you.

- There is no doubt that bland subjects tend to lead to bland evidence. Wherever possible, you should use material that you can get your teeth into. A subject that encourages a lot of argument or debate will generally give you lots of material to use, will be easier to research and will give you the opportunity to display your tact and sensitivity.

- Remember: You must not come up with any new system of indicating your evidence. You must use the referencing system given in the specification.

The most straightforward way to collect your evidence is to plan your progress through the evidence components. Negotiating and discussing a brief with your teacher and producing your Action Plan can be really useful.

- An Action Plan is not a requirement for your evidence in Communication Level 3 but it can be used as evidence for Improving Own Learning and Performance.

- It is also an excellent way of planning and keeping yourself on schedule. You will find an example of a blank Action Plan and a completed version in Appendix B (see pages 65–66).

- You can also use an Evidence Tracker like the one on page 39. It will allow you to fill in the components where you have completed work to the specification. It also shows how concise the portfolio should be. Quality, not quantity, is the secret.

C3.1a
(See Unit Specification on page 63.)

Taking part in a group discussion, which will give the quality of evidence required for Level 3 Communication, will mean that the topic for discussion has to be weighty and be one where you are likely to find a variety of opinions.

For example:

- A/S or A Level specifications may contain such topics as: why a particular war took place (History); look at the impact of population growth (Geography); consider the nature/nurture debate (Psychology); consider the impact of certain 'discoveries' on society (Science) and so on.

- Vocational A Level students often take business propositions and investigate their feasibility: this could produce your evidence. For example, they might be required to run a mini-enterprise or fund raise as part of their studies.

- Other topics that can be fruitful for group discussions are the sorts of issues that feature regularly in the press and on TV, for example:

  Cloning

  Surrogacy

  Blood sports

  Environmental issues

  Legislation on 'soft' drugs

  Immigration laws

There really are many topics that can provide the basis of an interesting discussion and on which people are likely to have some very diverse views.

- This discussion may be the opportunity for you to try out and test your ideas and opinions against those of other people. This should give you the chance to demonstrate that you can contribute and listen as appropriate and that you are sensitive to others' points of view.

Your evidence could include a Witness Testimony (see examples in Appendix C on pages 67–68) from an appropriate person, usually your teacher, to confirm that you have fulfilled the evidence requirements and covered all of the assessment criteria. That person must have sufficient knowledge of the Key Skills specification and be appropriately qualified to make that judgement. They must also include the context in which their observation took place. Witness testimonies should not be the sole form of evidence for discussion: there should be audio or video evidence that clearly shows the criteria being met. Your school/college might have facilities for students to video their own discussion; this may also be evidence for the Key Skill Working with Others.

C3.1b
(See Unit Specification on page 63.)

> To take this further you can prepare and present your topic to your class or tutor group. You must include at least one image to illustrate your point(s). (It may be that you begin to tackle C3.2 before C3.1a or C3.1b, as this will inform your opinion and arguments.)

- Look back at the earlier chapters for tips on how to make your presentation. In your planning, keep referring back to the specifications and make sure that you 'tweak' your presentation, if necessary, to fit the requirements.

- Using an IMAGE should not, at this level, present a problem. An image, in Key Skills speak, is something that is not verbal but which enhances the understanding of the audience, for example, charts, graphs, diagrams or photographs. The image can be one that you have created or it can be taken from an existing source. Do not forget to acknowledge where it came from.

- A range of alternative evidence can be used for this skill. It could include audio/video clips or assessor observation records **or** a Witness Testimony plus **either** audio/video recordings or supporting evidence, such as notes, prompt cards, OHTs etc.

C3.2 (See Unit Specification on page 63.)

> This is possibly the starting point for most students. This evidence will arise naturally from your 'research' into your topic, specifically your reading of **'two extended documents'** on **'complex' subjects**.

- The evidence in your portfolio could include the original reading list that you produce in order to investigate the topic.

- The documents you read must relate to a COMPLEX subject. You must remember this when making your selections. If you do not make appropriate choices, you will not be fulfilling the requirements of the specifications.

- You should identify quite clearly at least one image and make sure that your notes include your interpretation of this image.

- Keep checking the specification to make sure you are covering everything required.

- Look back to the discussion on note-taking earlier in this book and make sure that you are systematic and that you make quality notes. There is no need to word process notes – as long as they are legible they will suffice. For a moderator there is something a little suspicious about notes that seem to have all been word processed at the same time.

- Make sure that you put a date on your notes so that someone can follow your process and don't be afraid to go back and annotate or amend your notes.

- There is no need for a written outcome at this stage **but** you must include evidence that this reading and synthesis has taken place.

● Don't forget the impact of bias, both in your reading and your writing. Where you find it and recognise it, include that in your notes, so that the moderator can see you have that insight. Make your evidence obvious!

C3.3 (See Unit Specification on page 63.)

This evidence should follow smoothly if the above evidence requirements have been met. You will have had the opportunity to discuss and present your ideas with others. You will have all of the notes that you made as you researched the topic and now you should be well prepared to put pen to paper.

Earlier in this book there are some guidelines on how to prepare for an essay and for writing a report. These are probably the most straightforward approaches to fulfilling this evidence requirement.

● The essay could fit the requirements of an 'extended document' and include footnotes and a bibliography.

● You could also achieve the 'image' requirement by including data in the form of charts or graphs.

● An EXTENDED document would be at least three sides in length – Key Skills guidance says no more than that, but for most students this would represent between 750-1000 words handwritten.

● A report to your teacher could expand and develop the topic and bring in rather more of the material you have researched, which perhaps would not have been appropriate in the essay. This could also include charts or diagrams etc. in the appendices.

● In this book, essays and reports have been discussed, as they may well be the forms of writing that you are already undertaking in other subjects. There are, however, many other forms of extended document that could meet the specification.

TIP

You will not be able to produce all of this evidence at the correct level and quality without some practice. Discuss it with your teachers: they will have an idea of when you need to complete your portfolio of evidence in order that it can be moderated. This will give you a deadline. Please don't think that you can get this all out of the way in the first term of your studies. Perhaps you could put something together but the evidence you produce later in your studies will be of higher quality. This doesn't mean that you can't begin your planning, but rather see this as work in progress that you can go back and redraft/refine as necessary. You might even decide to try for a higher level Key Skill.

MAKING CONNECTIONS

By getting to know the Unit Specifications for all of your Key Skills you can start to make connections. Pieces of work that you use for evidence in one Key Skill may also cover some of the evidence requirements of another Key Skill.

Evidence you create for the section above may also cover:

LP	3.1	3.2	3.3
IT	3.1	3.2	3.3

★ See page 8 for further information on the wider Key Skills.
   Visit www.qca.org.uk for detailed Unit Specifications.

The external assessment

For some students, this will be the least worrying part of the Key Skills unit, as they will already feel well practised and comfortable with 'exams' and the idea of working under exam conditions.

- Do remember that you will not know the 'subject' of the test in the same way as sitting a GCSE in, say, Maths or French but, rather, you will be presented with material upon which you will demonstrate your Key Skills.

- The Communication Level 3 end assessment will assess your competence in Part A of the Unit Specification.

- As the new 2000 Key Skills are being phased in, there are only two or three opportunities a year to sit the end test. This will change as the qualification progresses and there is the intention that assessment will be available more or less on demand.

- You will need to speak with your teachers about the timing of your external assessment.

Exam technique

> Key Skills external assessments are no different from any other exam or time-constrained assessment. **You must do what you are asked in the time allowed.** Straightforward as this may sound, every year many students do not do this and are then surprised when they don't get the result they hoped for!

An example of a Communication Level 3 end test follows on page 45.

On the front cover of the document booklet it tells you:

WHAT YOU NEED:

- A resource document booklet – *supplied by the Board to your school.*
- This task booklet – *will tell you what to do with the document booklet.*
- An answer booklet – *although you can make notes on the other booklets, you write your answers here.*
- Pens with blue or black ink – *make sure you have a pen and that it works. A highlighter can come in useful.*

ADDITIONAL AIDS

- Dictionaries may not be used – *you will lose marks for poor spelling, punctuation and grammar.*

THERE ARE TWO PARTS TO THIS PAPER

Part 1 – Short answer questions (25 marks)

Part 2 – Extended answer questions (25 marks)

This should suggest that both parts carry equal weighting and that it will probably be useful to divide your time equally between Parts A and B.

TIME ALLOWED – 1 HOUR 30 MINUTES. THIS INCLUDES READING TIME.

To complete this activity successfully you will need to:

- read the information supplied in the task booklet and resource booklet. *How is your reading speed? Can you read quickly and synthesise this information? Would a highlighter pen help to illuminate key points as you read through?*

- complete both parts of the paper. *Manage your time. When half of the time is gone, move on to Part B even if you haven't finished Part A — you can always go back.*

- write all the answers in your answer book. *Remember if you do run short of time — which you shouldn't — the examiner will probably give you some marks for notes to show how you were going to develop your argument if you had time. It is a good idea to jot a plan down at the start so that when you are getting tired you can refer back to it.*

Approaching the questions

The best thing you can do is to always turn over the paper and quickly scan through the questions — do not write at this stage.

The questions

- There are four questions in Part A and one question in Part B. There are 25 marks for each section and therefore we can assume that both sections carry equal weighting.

- This should straightaway tell you that your time should be split equally between Part A and Part B.

- If you allow yourself 15 minutes for reading and planning, you will have just over 30 minutes each for Part A and Part B.

- Remember this and monitor your progress.

The source material

There are two documents, one that seems more like an article or report, which includes some graphs, and the other taken from a book by Germaine Greer.

- Skim through the documents quickly, getting a general sense of what they are saying.

- After you have done this, go through them systematically and highlight the main points and statistics.

- It is quicker to use a highlighter pen to mark key points than to make notes on a separate sheet or on the paper. You should, however, use whichever method you feel comfortable with.

- When you have synthesised the material and identified the key points, then you can begin to answer the questions.

Now, find a quiet place where you will not be disturbed for an hour and a half, and answer the End Test.

When you have finished, go and have a soft drink or a coffee and then you will be ready to come back to check YOUR answers against the model answers in Chapter 7, pages 56–59.

The Exemplar Test

LEVEL	PAPER
Key Skills – Level 3	Communication

WHAT YOU NEED:

- a resource document booklet;
- this task booklet;
- an answer booklet;
- pens with black or blue ink.

THERE ARE TWO PARTS TO THIS PAPER:

Part 1 – Short answer questions (25 marks)

Part 2 – Extended answer questions (25 marks)

ADDITIONAL AIDS

- dictionaries may not be used

TIME ALLOWED – 1 HOUR 30 MINUTES. THIS INCLUDES READING TIME.

To complete this activity successfully you will need to:

- read the information supplied in the task booklet and the resource booklet;
- complete both parts of the paper;
- write all answers in your answer booklet.

Instructions to candidates

- Write your personal details in the spaces provided on the answer booklet.

- Do not open this task booklet until you are told to do so by the supervisor.

- Read each question carefully and attempt all questions.

- Write in black or blue ink only.

- Make sure you write legibly in the spaces provided.

- Make sure your meaning is clear.

- If you use extra paper make sure that it has your name and candidate number on it and is attached securely to the answer booklet.

- At the end of the assessment hand your resource booklet, task booklet, your answer booklet and all notes to the supervisor.

PART 1 SHORT ANSWER QUESTIONS

Refer to **both** documents when answering the questions.

1. Suggest <u>six</u> pieces of evidence from the document that women are discriminated against in the workplace.

[7 marks]

2. Using your own words, list obstacles women can face when working on trying to gain promotion.

[5 marks]

3. What does the writer of Document 2 think of equality and Equal Opportunities legislation? Compare her views to those of the author of Document 1 [commenting also on how tone, vocabulary and style of writing are used to convey those views].

[8 marks]

4. In your own words, summarise the views of the two writers on how discrimination against women can be resolved.

[5 marks]

PART 2 EXTENDED ANSWER QUESTION

5. Write a detailed response to the author of DOCUMENT 2 explaining why you either agree or disagree with the views put forward in her article. You may include information from Documents 1 and 2 in your answer. You should write about 150 – 200 words.

[25 marks]

Communication

Level 3

External Assessment

SOURCE MATERIALS

To be used with short answer and extended answer questions.

DOCUMENT 1

Majority trapped by glass ceiling

Despite laws to prevent discrimination against women, they still have a raw deal within a system dominated by men.

THERE are more British women than men: 51% of the population is female. This is because women live on average 6 years longer than men and boys are more likely to die at birth than girls.

Although women form a majority of the population, they make up a minority of Britain's decision makers. Under 7% of members of parliament and only 0.5% of directors of private companies are women.

The position of women in society has changed a great deal since 1900. Before World War II only a third of the workforce was female and women were expected to stay at home. Because of the war, from 1941 women aged 20 – 30 without children were required to work in factories and services to replace men who had left to join the armed forces. At the end of the war women were encouraged to give up their jobs to make way for the men returning from war. Since the 1960s, however, the number of working women has increased. By 2001 women will make up an estimated 45% of the workforce.

But men continue to hold the most highly-paid and influential positions in government and industry. Over 70% of working women hold the lowest-paid jobs. Only 10% of senior managers are female.

One report concluded that "for too many women there is a glass ceiling over their aspirations – it allows them to see where they might go, but stops them getting there."

For more than 20 years, successive governments have tried to prevent sex discrimination (eg. Equal Pay Act 1970 established equal pay for the same work). Nevertheless, many women are still paid 25 – 40% less than men doing equivalent work.

Some jobs are not open to women at all. Women cannot hold certain positions within the armed forces, for example.

According to the Equal Opportunities Commission (EOC), hidden barriers prevent women from securing top jobs. Some employers still believe women are less capable of making decisions. This is not borne out by the facts. At all levels of education women perform well, and some better than men. Girls do better at GCSE and, at university, obtain as many 1st class degrees as men.

But women face an even greater hurdle than employers: they also perform most of the work involved in caring for children and for older and disabled people. Most of Britain's carers are women – the "invisible" work force because it is largely unpaid and doesn't appear on economic records. Parliament itself is one example of the difficulties women face in combining family commitments and paid work. Since women got the vote in 1918 and until the election this year (1997), only 140 or so had become MPs. This was partly because few women were selected as candidates. But it was also because politicians' working hours conflict with family life. "Late hours deter women from seeking entry into Parliament," said one woman MP. "This makes the House of Commons profoundly unrepresentative of a nation composed of almost 52% women."

Of course, the election of so many Labour Party women MPs has changed all this quite dramatically. Perhaps, even in politics, gender is becoming less of an issue.

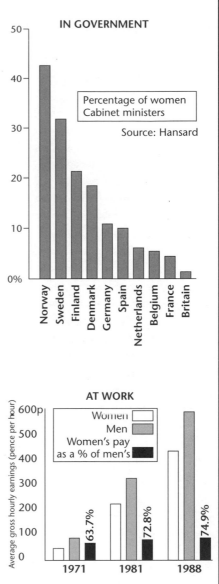

IN GOVERNMENT

Percentage of women Cabinet ministers

Source: Hansard

(Norway, Sweden, Finland, Denmark, Germany, Spain, Netherlands, Belgium, France, Britain)

AT WORK

Average gross hourly earnings (pence per hour)

Women
Men
Women's pay as a % of men's

1971: 63.7%
1981: 72.8%
1988: 74.9%

The struggle to survive

Long hours of hard work are a necessity for many women, especially in the developing world.

IN many countries in Africa and Asia women are the main farmers: they till the land, sow the seeds and tend the crops. They also perform most of the housework.

Aid charities say that women form an essential, but largely ignored, part of the economy of developing countries. Studies suggest that often the work undertaken by women is harder than that done by men and involves working longer hours than they do. A study in Tanzania, for example, showed that women work 3,069 hours per year compared with 1,829 for men.

According to the United Nations women grow more than half the food produced in developing countries: over 80% for sub-Sahara Africa. Women collect most of the water needed for families and crops.

In some families, women are in charge of all the farming work because the men have migrated to the towns in search of paid jobs. A third of all rural households in developing countries are headed by women.

A study by Oxfam in Nepal found that females tend to perform more work than males from an early age. Girls rarely go to school because they have to look after younger brothers and sisters or help their mother. As a result, as few as 18% of all Nepalese women can read compared with 52% of boys.

There is a growing trend also for females to migrate to towns in search of factory work. Clothing factories in the Philippines, for example, employ 90% female labour. Most women work for just 2 or 3 years in the factories partly because the work is so wearing.

Other women in towns earn their living on the "informal market". This means they have no regular paid work but make ends meet selling goods on the street or doing odd jobs.

Feminism, the fight for women's rights, is often seen as a western ideology which is a luxury for poor women in developing countries.

Family

Women with young children tend to take a break from work or work part-time. But having children does not affect the working patterns of men so dramatically.

Only 8% of mothers with children aged 0-4 years are in full-time work and 21% in part-time work.

83% of fathers with young children are in full-time work and 1% in part-time work.

DOCUMENT 2

Based on 'The Whole Woman' by Germaine Greer (publishers – Doubleday 1999)

The notion of equality takes the male status quo as the condition to which women aspire. Men live and work in a frighteningly unfree and tyrannical society, constructed upon the oppression of junior males by senior ones. … As soon as a woman enters a male preserve, be it the police, the military, the building site, the law, the clergy, she finds herself in an alien and repellent world which changes her fundamentally even as she struggles to exert the smallest influence on it. Aspirants to rank in such groups have to learn the ropes and then bounce their rivals on to them. The woman who becomes leader of a conventional political party can only do so because she has become tougher than the men in it. It was often said of Margaret Thatcher that, despite her frothy bows and four-inch heels, she was the only man in her cabinet.

The Wilson government of 1975 that brought in the Sex Discrimination Act along with the Equal Opportunities Commission was made up of businessmen and lawyers. The Sex Discrimination Act was designed to give people the illusion that women's oppression had been recognised and that something was being done about it and, at the same time, to reassure that no great changes were likely to ensue and business would go on exactly as usual. There was never the remotest chance that employers would find themselves facing expensive adjustments to wages policy even though the Act would create thousands of hours of lucrative work for lawyers as case after case was argued interminably only to be lost.

For the young women who now outnumber young men graduating in law, life in chambers can be a nightmare of discrimination amounting to outright persecution and harassment. A report by legal recruitment consultants Reynell, published in January 1997, found that a quarter of women solicitors have suffered sexual harassment and almost half have been disadvantaged because of discrimination on grounds of sex. Yet women lawyers seldom bring cases under the Sex Discrimination Act. As lawyers they know better. In their struggle to build a career, even if the woman lawyers won their cases, they would lose their prospects.

Every week brings new evidence of the struggles of women in male-dominated professions. The solution, some say, is to have equal numbers of women. This cannot be done because women will not be recruited in large numbers unless a policy of reverse discrimination is adopted. This cannot happen because it is illegal under the Sex Discrimination Act to allocate resources or jobs to women as it can be argued that this discriminated against men. Equality is cruel to women because it requires them to copy behaviours that they find profoundly alien and disturbing. If women can see no future beyond joining the masculine elite on its own terms, our civilization will become more destructive than ever. Women need liberation, not equality. They should be free to define their own values, order their own priorities and decide their own fate.

How did you do?

When you have finished the End Test, compare your answers to the model answers in Chapter 7, pages 56–59.

It is probably easier to judge your performance in Part A, as to some extent the questions are shorter and more straightforward. However, you should be able to get a feel for the style of the end test and whether you are comfortable with this type of assessment.

You will have plenty of opportunities over the coming months to further develop your Key Skills. Use this book to guide you and work with your teachers and fellow students to make the most of every opportunity to develop your Key Skills – you may be surprised at what you can achieve!

Good Luck!

Airlines conceal attacks on crew

Linear notes

Main point of article: Attacks against airline crews are considerably higher than officially recorded.

★ Official BA statistics Oct 98-Mar 99 = 122 incidents

★ BA confidential report = 644 incidents

★ BA systems allow crews to report incidents in confidence

★ Government survey – CAA statistics 800 incidents in 7 months, 1:870 flights

★ BA report 1:440 flights

★ Spokesman – reason: availability of alcohol while waiting for flights

★ BA offer crew insurance, counselling and training in handling aggressive passengers

★ Legislation – abuse to aircraft crew, 2 years imprisonment + £5000 fine

Mind Map

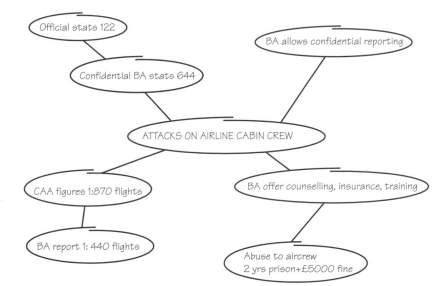

Airbag kills driver in 19 mph crash

Linear notes

★ 47 year old Merseyside woman first airbag fatality

★ Car travelling at 19 mph

★ Driver of other car minor injuries, victim fatal head wound

★ Doctors say victim sitting too close to airbag

★ Airbag injuries more common in US

★ US airbags protect unbelted passengers/UK airbags protect from steering wheel

★ US 145 fatalities from airbags inc 84 children; common factor too close

★ Doctors know airbags in UK can produce minor injuries but warn of increases

★ Soc of Motor Manufacturers & Traders say do not disconnect airbags

★ AA – death was freak accident

★ New "Smart" airbags will adjust to the passenger

Mind Map

Best ways to pay for your operations

Linear notes

★ 1000s on NHS waiting lists

★ Medical insurance costs rising

★ 1999 – 160,000 people pay for surgery in private hospitals

★ Main hospitals similar charges for standard procedures

★ Cataracts £1300-2600. Varicose veins £975-1500, Hip replacements £5000-7800

★ Some procedures very costly e.g. heart bypass £12.5k

★ Hospital groups offer credit cards and finance

★ New generation of health insurance, high excess/low cost

★ People can use ISAs to save tax free and then use for medical bills

Mind Map

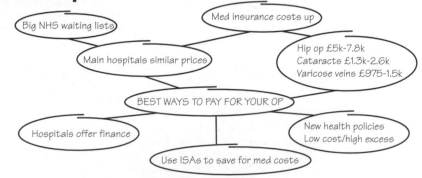

How to write an essay

An example of how you might plan your essay on the 'The commercial benefits of genetically modified food far outweigh any health risks'

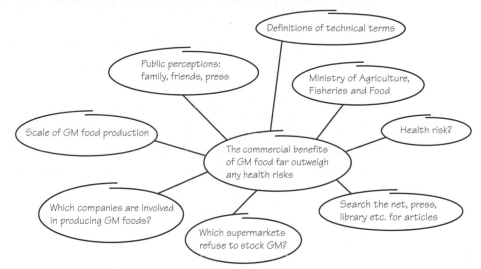

Your essay plan might look something like this:

1. INTRODUCTION
   Definitions of GM etc.
   State what the essay will do/show
2. MAIN BODY
   - Public opinion
   - Official government response
   - Manufacturers of GM food response
   - Supermarkets' attitudes to GM foods
   - Any other relevant materials
3. CONCLUSION
4. REFERENCES AND BIBLIOGRAPHY

Even without the 'meat' on the 'bones', a simple plan can make life much easier. You know what to do and you are not working aimlessly. Many students waste time by not preparing in this way. You would not drive in a foreign country and try to reach a specific destination without reading a map – think of your essay plan in that way. It is the **route** that you will take.

Writing a report

An example of how you might plan your report on the usage of your school canteen

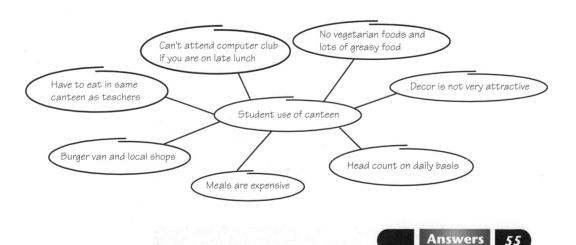

Without much research you can perhaps imagine that in many schools, some or all of the above may apply to our hypothetical canteen problems.

A first plan for your report might be like this:

- TITLE – Investigation into the use of the school canteen
- CONTENTS (this will come later)
- INTRODUCTION (write this later)
- MAIN BODY
1. Head count – need to research actual figures for use
2. Meals considered expensive – breakdown of costs needed, perhaps write to LEA
3. Not much healthy food – need to get balance between healthy items and fast food
4. Burger vans and local shops – investigate what they provide and cost
5. Staff in canteen – interview staff and students about this issue
6. Decor of canteen – speak to School Governors and/or LEA
7. Timing of lunch break – speak to head teacher
- CONCLUSIONS
- RECOMMENDATIONS
- APPENDICES

This would now give you a really clear framework of what you need to do and how to make progress. You do not need to wait to the end to start writing. If you have a plan, you can write to your plan.

Exemplar Test – Part A

You are required to refer to both documents when answering Part A.

> 1. **Suggest six pieces of evidence from the document that women are discriminated against in the workplace. (7 marks)**

This question assesses the skills **3.2.1** and **3.2.2**, your ability to **'read and synthesise information from two extended documents about a complex subject. One of these documents should include at least one image.'**

The evidence reference numbers have been broken down further to guide you. In your portfolio, however, you should keep to the original reference numbers (3.1, 3.2, 3.3).

You can pick up some tips from this as this test paper gives you:

A **examples of what the Board consider to be EXTENDED and COMPLEX documents**

B **examples of IMAGES, in this instance bar charts**

In order to score the maximum points on this question, you would need to include the following:

3.2.1 Evidence that you have read and selected material from Documents 1 and 2. (1 mark)

3.2.2 At least six of the following major points made in the documents:

★ Less than 7% of women are MPs.

★ Women make up only 0.5% of directors of Plc's.

★ 70%+ of women hold lowest paid jobs.

★ Only 10% of senior managers are women.

★ Women's wages are up to 40% less than men doing equivalent work.

★ By 1997 still only 140+ MPs were women.

★ Reynell Report – high level of sexual harassment and discrimination against women solicitors (1997).

★ Hansard Graph – Britain has lowest number of women cabinet ministers.

★ Women's working patterns affected by childcare. 8% of mothers with small children work full-time, 83% of fathers work full-time.

(1 mark per point – maximum 6 marks)

> **2. Using your own words, list obstacles women can face when working or trying to gain promotion. (5 marks)**

This question assesses your ability to use skills **3.2.1**, **3.2.2** and **3.2.3**.

3.2.1 Evidence that you have read and selected material from Documents 1 and 2. (1 mark)

3.2.2 You should comment on at least three of the following things that can influence women at work:

★ The attitude of some employers towards women.

★ The impact of childcare and other household and family commitments.

★ The structure of the working day and its impact on women's lives.

★ Sexual harassment, discrimination etc. from male colleagues.

(1 mark per point – maximum 3 marks)

3.2.3 You must express these points in your own words – demonstrating that you have understood what you have read.

Note: Although the question uses the word 'list', it is not sufficient to write out a list. The examining board expect you to link up your ideas using appropriate language and showing a logical sequence.

> **3. What does the writer of Document 2 think of equality and Equal Opportunities legislation? Compare her views to those of the author of Document 1 (commenting also on how tone, vocabulary and style of writing are used to convey those views). (8 marks)**

3.2.2 This question requires you to identify the main points from Document 2, which should include:

★ In order to succeed, women have to behave like men.

★ In many cases women have to be more 'macho' than men.

★ Encouraging women to behave like men is destructive to society.

★ Legislation and the law work to the advantage of men and lawyers; they have not changed women's lives.

★ Legislation is a costly route to follow and can put further obstacles in woman's way.

★ Sex discrimination cannot be countered by reverse discrimination, as that would be illegal.

(1 mark per point – maximum 3 marks)

Comparing Documents 1 and 2

★ Statistics show that even though as capable as men, women tend to be worse paid and in less responsible jobs.

★ The position of women in the workforce is illustrated by statistics.

(Maximum 2 marks for identifying factual content)

Comparison of style of writing, vocabulary and tone – full marks can only be gained if you show comparison, for example, using 'whereas', 'on the other hand' etc., when linking your points.

Document 1

★ Uses a report style, is neutral, as far as we can tell is factual and accepts that equality is a possibility.

Document 2

★ Gives opinions, is personal and argumentative, using forceful language, and puts forward an argument through examples: equality is not possible, probable or desirable.

(A maximum of 3 marks)

> **4. In your own words, summarise the views of the two writers on how discrimination against women can be resolved. (5 marks)**

3.2.2 You need to demonstrate here that you have identified the main lines of argument used in Documents I and 2.

★ Document I accepts the view that sex discrimination can be resolved by the inclusion of equal numbers of men and women in the workforce.

★ Document I also assumes that by increasing the number of women MPs, things will improve for women generally.

★ In Document 2, the writer argues that equality is not a solution and that only liberation will improve women's lives.

(Maximum of 2 marks per document – maximum total 4 marks)

3.3.2 The answer should be clear and structured.

(I mark)

Exemplar Test – Part B

> **5. Write a detailed response to the author of Document 2 explaining why you either agree or disagree with the views put forward in her article. You may include information from Documents 1 and 2 in your answer. You should write about 150-200 words. (25 marks))**

As long as you answer the question, you can answer in any suitable form, for example, a letter, an e-mail, a newspaper article or a more usual essay-style answer.

3.3.1 You need to demonstrate an appropriate style through your use of:

★ vocabulary

★ tone

★ structure of your sentences

(A mark for each – maximum of 3 marks)

3.3.2 You should use paragraphs and link information and ideas in an ordered way.

(A maximum of 2 marks)

3.2.3 These marks are for the synthesis of ideas and key information from the documents. You should present your case relevant to your purpose.

(A maximum of 8 marks)

3.3.2 In order to gain maximum marks you should go further than 3.2.3 above and be able to argue logically and in depth. A high quality answer will include a conclusion.

(A maximum of 5 marks)

3.3.3 Above all your text must be legible.

(1 mark)

You can score on one of the three levels below, depending upon the quality of your work:

★ You spell, punctuate and use the rules of grammar with reasonable accuracy; you include a range of specialist terms where appropriate. (1-2 marks)

Or

★ You spell, punctuate and use the rules of grammar with considerable accuracy; you include a good range of specialist terms. (3-4 marks)

Or

★ You spell, punctuate and use the rules of grammar with almost faultless accuracy, you deploy a range of grammar constructions and you use a wide range of specialist terms with precision. (5-6 marks)

(A maximum of 7 marks)

(With thanks to the QCA for granting permission to reproduce materials and for use of the marking scheme.)

This is a model answer for Part B, question 5. Check your own answer against it. Remember that it does not have to be identical but should contain an argument using the evidence of the texts.

Germaine Greer, in Document 2, argues that equality for women should not mean accepting a 'male status quo', which would therefore define women's equality for them. This would seem to be relinquishing one form of oppression only to be bound by another and suggests that maybe class and age differentials are also important factors in oppression with our social behaviour.

The author is equally dismissive of legislation designed to tackle inequality. She suggests that legislation leads women to believe that their cause has validity and that the law will support them. By examining the statistics presented in Document 1, it is clear how few women hold positions of power either in the workforce or in the political arena, despite 30 years of legislation. Greer makes the point that the only group to benefit from legislation are lawyers, again a male preserve.

Women's liberation seems to be the only true way for women to be free from a male hegemony, where the only well paid work is men's work and the contribution of women to the economy through caring, nurturing and childcare is undervalued and ignored. However, it is difficult to see how this can change as women have so little access to the existing decision-making institutions, despite nearly 80 years of emancipation.

Appendices

A Communication Level 3 – Unit Specification

B Action Plans – including a completed version

C Witness Testimonies – including a completed version

D Proxy Qualifications

E Where to find out more

KEY SKILLS UNIT

Communication

What is this unit about?

This unit is about applying your communication skills to deal with complex subjects and extended written material.

You will show you can:

- contribute to discussions;
- make a presentation;
- read and synthesise information;
- write different types of documents.

How do I use the information in this unit?

There are three parts to the unit: what you need to know, what you must do and guidance.

Part A
WHAT YOU NEED TO KNOW

This part of the unit tells you what you need to learn and practise to feel confident about applying communication skills in your studies, work or other aspects of your life.

Part B
WHAT YOU MUST DO

This part of the unit describes the skills you must show. All your work for this section will be assessed. You must have evidence that you can do all the things listed in the bullet points.

Part C
GUIDANCE

This part describes some activities you might like to use to develop and show your communication skills. It also contains examples of the sort of evidence you could produce to prove you have the skills required.

LEVEL 3

Part A

WHAT YOU NEED TO KNOW

In discussions,

YOU NEED TO KNOW HOW TO:

- vary how and when you participate to suit your purpose *(eg to present a complicated line of reasoning or argument, explain events, express opinions and ideas)* and the situation *(eg formality, nature of the group)*;

- listen and respond sensitively *(eg acknowledge gender and cultural aspects, how others might be feeling)* and develop points and ideas;

- make openings to encourage others to contribute *(eg invite others to speak, ask follow-up questions to encourage people to develop points)*.

In making a presentation,

YOU NEED TO KNOW HOW TO:

- prepare the presentation to suit your purpose *(eg present an argument in a debate, findings from an investigation, outcomes from a design brief)*;

- match your language and style to suit the complexity of the subject, the formality of the situation and the needs of the audience *(eg confidently use standard English, precisely use vocabulary)*;

- structure what you say *(eg help listeners follow the sequence of main points, ideas)*;

- use techniques to engage the audience, including images *(eg give examples to illustrate complex points, relate what is said to audience experience, vary tone of voice, use images, such as charts, pictures and models to illustrate points)*.

In reading and synthesising information,

YOU NEED TO KNOW HOW TO:

- find and skim read extended documents, such as text books, secondary sources, articles and reports, to identify relevant material *(eg to extend thinking around a subject, obtain evidence, opinions and ideas)*;

- scan and read the material to find the specific information you need;

- use appropriate sources of reference to help you understand complex lines of reasoning and information from text and images *(eg consult databases and other texts, ask others for clarification)*;

- compare accounts and recognise opinion and possible bias *(eg identify the writer's intentions by the way meaning and information is conveyed)*;

- synthesise the information you have obtained for a purpose *(eg present your own interpretation of the subject in a way that brings information together in a coherent form for a report or presentation)*.

In writing documents,

YOU NEED TO KNOW HOW TO:

- select appropriate forms for presenting information *(eg extended essay or report, images, such as pictures, charts and diagrams)* to suit your purpose *(eg present an argument, ideas, a complicated line of reasoning or a series of events)*;

- select appropriate styles to suit the degree of formality required and nature of the subject *(eg use vocabulary, sentence structures and tone that suit the intended readers and the complexity or sensitivity of the subject)*;

- organise material coherently *(eg use paragraphs, headings, sub-headings, indentation and highlighting, link information and ideas in an ordered way using words such as 'however', 'therefore')*;

- make meaning clear by writing, proof-reading and re-drafting documents so that spelling, punctuation and grammar are accurate.

Part B

WHAT YOU MUST DO

You must:

Evidence must show you can:

C3.1a

Contribute to a group discussion about a complex subject.

- make clear and relevant contributions in a way that suits your purpose and situation;
- listen and respond sensitively to others, and develop points and ideas; and
- create opportunities for others to contribute when appropriate.

C3.1b

Make a presentation about a complex subject, using at least **one** image to illustrate complex points.

- speak clearly and adapt your style of presentation to suit your purpose, subject, audience and situation;
- structure what you say so that the sequence of information and ideas may be easily followed; and
- use a range of techniques to engage the audience, including effective use of images.

C3.2

Read and synthesise information from **two** extended documents about a complex subject.

One of these documents should include at least **one** image.

- select and read material that contains the information you need;
- identify accurately, and compare, the lines of reasoning and main points from texts and images; and
- synthesise the key information in a form that is relevant to your purpose.

C3.3

Write **two** different types of documents about complex subjects.

One piece of writing should be an extended document and include at least **one** image.

- select and use a form and style of writing that is appropriate to your purpose and complex subject matter;
- organise relevant information clearly and coherently, using specialist vocabulary when appropriate; and
- ensure your text is legible and your spelling, grammar and punctuation are accurate, so your meaning is clear.

Part C

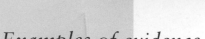

GUIDANCE

Examples of activities you might use

You will have opportunities to develop and use your communication skills during your studies, work or other activities. For example, when:

- planning and researching a project or assignment;
- carrying out an investigation and reporting findings;
- dealing with customers or clients;
- exchanging information and ideas with work colleagues or other students.

You will need time to practise your skills and prepare for assessment. So it is important to plan ahead.

In preparing your presentation, you may read about the subject and produce handouts. These could also be used as evidence of your reading and writing skills. If available, you could use IT to produce written material and images, such as a graph or chart.

You will need to think about the quality of your communication skills and check your evidence covers all the requirements in Part B.

Examples of evidence

3.1a DISCUSSION

A record from an assessor who has observed your discussion and noted how you met the requirements of the unit, or an audio/video tape of the discussion.

3.1b PRESENTATION

A record from an assessor who has observed your presentation or an audio/video tape.

Notes from preparing and making your presentation with a copy of the image used.

3.2 READING

A record of what you read and why, including a note or copy of the images. Notes, highlighted text or answers to questions about the material you read. Evidence of synthesising information could be handouts for your presentation.

3.3 WRITING

Two different documents might include an extended essay or report, with an image such as a chart, graph or diagram and a business letter or memo.

If producing certain types of evidence creates difficulties, through disability or for another reason, you may be able to use other ways to show your achievement. Ask your tutor or supervisor for further information.

This unit is for use in programmes starting from September 2000.

QCA/99/342   First published 1999 ISBN 1 85838 402 8

Copyright © 1999 Qualifications and Curriculum Authority.

Printed in Great Britain.

The Qualifications and Curriculum Authority is an exempt charity under Schedule 2 of the Charities Act 1993.

Qualifications and Curriculum Authority, 29 Bolton Street, London W1Y 7PD. www.qca.org.uk   Chairman: Sir William Stubbs.

Copies of this document may be obtained using the QCA *Publications List and Order Form* or by contacting: QCA Publications, PO Box 99, Sudbury, Suffolk, CO10 6SN. Telephone: 01787 884444, Fax: 01787 312950. When ordering, please quote title and reference number.

Key Skills Action Plan

NAME:

DATE:

KEY SKILL:

LEVEL:

DATE	Planned Tasks	Review Date	Completed Date	Evidence Component	Check links with other Key Skills

Student Signature

Tutor Signature

Date

Key Skills Action Plan

NAME: Jon Evans

DATE: 7 September 2000

KEY SKILL: Communication

LEVEL: 3

DATE	Planned Tasks	Review Date	Completed Date	Evidence Component	Check links with other Key Skills
7/9	Go to library to find sources for GM food project	14/9	11/9	3.2	IT 3.1, LP 3.1 3.2
	Speak with Mr Ross in staff room to see if I'm on the right track				
11/9	Use private study time to write to supermarkets about the GM food policy	8/10	7/11	3.2/3.3	IT 3.2,3.3 LP 3.2
17/9	Design questionnaire to ask family and friends about GM foods	1/10			IT 3.1,3.2,3.3
23/11	Meeting with Mr Ross to discuss progress to date and explain how I will take this work forward		23/11		LP 3.3

Student Signature *J. Evans*

Tutor Signature *P. Ross*　　　　Date *27/11/2000*

N.B. **Action Plans are not required** as evidence for **Key Skill Communication,** but they are a really good way for students to keep a track of the work they are doing and make **LINKS** with other **Key Skills**

WITNESS TESTIMONY

Student Name: **Key Skill:**

EVIDENCE COMPONENT OBSERVED:

DESCRIPTION OF ACTIVITY:
DATE ACTIVITY TOOK PLACE:
CONTEXT:

How did the candidate meet the requirements of the Unit Specification?

Continue overleaf if necessary.

WITNESS SIGNATURE:
WITNESS STATUS:

Contact Address
Tel:
DATE:

Student Signature

Date:

WITNESS TESTIMONY

Student Name: Jane Arthur

Key Skill: Communication

EVIDENCE COMPONENT OBSERVED: 3.1a

DESCRIPTION OF ACTIVITY: Group Discussion on charity fundraising
DATE ACTIVITY TOOK PLACE: 24 November 2000
CONTEXT: Jane is one of 8 students in my tutor group undertaking the school 'Good Neighbours' programme in which the students contribute to the local community. This group had had a preliminary meeting and decided they would like to fund raise for the local hospice. The discussion was convened by the students themselves to take this forward.

How did the candidate meet the requirements of the Unit Specification?
Jane was very active in organising this meeting and at the outset offered to take the Chair. She had produced a short agenda and a list of decisions which had to be taken. This was agreed by the rest of the group. The subject of the discussion was COMPLEX, it involved the students in research into the nature of the conditions suffered by the patients using the hospice.

Jane had used the Internet to find out more information about some forms of childhood cancer and she presented this information to the meeting.

She was particularly sensitive to two other members of the group who have had personal experience of relatives or friends staying at the hospice. On more than one occasion Jane invited these students to help the group to understand the need for fund raising and how this can help the hospice. Jane was SENSITIVE and responsive to the rest of the group and ensured that when someone had a point to make they were listened to.

On at least 2 occasions Jane brought the discussion back on course by summing up what had been decided and making suggestions on how to take this forward.

By the end of the meeting the group had discussed the setting up and financing of a charity stall on the market, contacting the local authority concerning permits needed, arranging another meeting with the Senior Officer at the hospice and placing orders for goods for the stall. Jane was delegated to type up the minutes.

SUPPORTING EVIDENCE IS ON VIDEO NO. 7

Continue overleaf if necessary.

WITNESS SIGNATURE: Ann Jones
WITNESS STATUS: Pastoral Tutor

Contact Address Newtown College, Newtown
Tel: 01566 879923
DATE: 24/11/2000

Student Signature *J. Arthur*

Date: *27/11/2000*

D Proxy Qualifications

Details of proxy qualifications to act as exemptions from parts of the Key Skills Qualification. Parts A and B apply.

Part A (External Assessment)

English Language or Literature, Gaelic and Welsh, and Communication

Mathematics[1] and Application of Number

GCE AS/A Level A-E examination performance provides exemption for the external test in these Key Skills at Level 3.

GCSE A*-C examination performance provides exemption for the external test in these Key Skills at Level 2.

GCSE D-G examination performance provides exemption for the external test in these Key Skills at Level 1.

Computing[1] or ICT[1] and Information Technology

GCE A Level A-E performance provides full exemption for the Key Skill at Level 3.

GCE AS A-E performance provides exemption for the external test in the Key Skill at Level 3.

GCSE A*-C performance provides full exemption for the Key Skill at Level 2.

GCSE D-G performance provides full exemption for the Key Skill at Level 1.

GCSE Short Course ICT[1] and Information Technology

A*-C performance provides exemption for the external test in the Key Skill at Level 2 and also for one of the two specified purposes of the internal Key Skill component at Level 2.

D-G performance provides exemption for the external test in the Key Skill at Level 1 and also for one of the two specified purposes of the internal Key Skill component at Level 1.

Part Award, Single Award or Double Award in Vocational A Level and GNVQ or Part One GNVQ in ICT[1] and Information Technology

Vocational AS/A Level (Advanced GNVQ) A-E performance provides full exemption for the Key Skill at Level 3.

Intermediate GNVQ or Part One GNVQ Pass/Merit/Distinction performance provides full exemption for the Key Skill at Level 2.

Foundation GNVQ or Part One GNVQ Pass/Merit/Distinction performance provides full exemption for the Key Skill at Level 1.

The currency of qualification specifications

The above exemptions have been confirmed for those specifications accredited by the regulatory authorities. Revision to accredited specifications would result in the exemptions offered by that subject being reviewed and if necessary revised or removed.

The currency of examination performance

The currency of exemptions provided by proxy qualifications must be no longer than three years from the date of award to the date of claim. In these circumstances, exemptions from September 2000 can only be claimed for qualifications gained after September 1997.

[1] This applies to all qualifications whether gained through the medium of English, Gaelic or Welsh

Part B (Portfolio)

NATIONAL QUALIFICATIONS FRAMEWORK

The following titles for English, Mathematics and ICT Qualifications provide exemptions to the external assessment of the Key Skills.

For the Communication Key Skill

ENGLISH

GCSE English

GCSE English Literature

GCE AS and Advanced English Language

GCE AS and Advanced English Language and Literature

For the Application of Number Key Skill

MATHEMATICS

GCSE Mathematics

GCE AS or GCE Advanced Mathematics

GCE AS or GCE Advanced Pure Mathematics

GCE AS or GCE Advanced Further Mathematics

GCE AS or GCE Advanced Statistics

GCE AS Mechanics

GCE AS Discrete Mathematics

GCE AS Applied Mathematics

For the IT Key Skill

ICT

GCSE IT

GCSE (Short Course) ICT

GCE AS ICT

GCE AS Computing

GCE A ICT

GCE A Computing

GNVQ Foundation ICT (6-unit award)

GNVQ Foundation ICT (3-unit award)

GNVQ Intermediate ICT (6-unit award)

GNVQ Intermediate ICT (3-unit award)

GNVQ Advanced ICT (12-unit award)

GNVQ Advanced ICT (6-unit award)

GNVQ Advanced ICT (3-unit award)

E   Where to find out more

Useful websites

Association of Colleges (AoC)
www.aoc.co.uk

BBC Further Education
www.bbc.co.uk/education/fe
www.bbc.co.uk/education/fe/skills/index.shtml

Department for Education and Employment
www.dfee.gov.uk
If you are involved in producing a Progress File you can gain help from
www.dfee.gov.uk/progfile/index.htm

Further Education Development Agency (FEDA) – the main body leading Key Skills
developments in schools and colleges.
www.feda.ac.uk

For **GNVQ support** try
www.feda.ac.uk/gnvq

National Extension College (NEC) – produces useful material to support Key Skills
development.
www.nec.ac.uk/index.html

Qualifications and Curriculum Authority (QCA) – the organisation responsible for the
development, implementation and quality assurance of all national qualifications.
www.qca.org.uk

University and Colleges Admissions Service (UCAS)
www.ucas.ac.uk

Letts Educational
www.letts-education.com